Looking Ahead
Independent School Issues & Answers

Edited by
Patrick F. Bassett &
Louis M. Crosier

1994
Avocus Publishing, Inc.
Washington, D.C.

LOOKING AHEAD:
INDEPENDENT SCHOOL ISSUES & ANSWERS

Edited by Patrick F. Bassett &
Louis M. Crosier

Published by:

Avocus Publishing, Inc.
1223 Potomac Street, NW
Washington, DC 20007 U.S.A.
(202) 333–8190
FAX: (202) 337–3809
Orders: 800–345–6665

Disclaimer:

To my family, my best teachers, all.
— P.F. Bassett

To my grandfather, with love.
— L.M. Crosier

Contents

v

Preface

How to Use this Book

Looking Ahead: Independent School Issues & Answers is the third book in Avocus' independent school trilogy. Its goal is to advance the discussion on improving independent day school life by involving all faculty, trustees, parents, administrators and student leaders in the discussion of contemporary independent school issues.

Just as the self-evaluation and accreditation process provide faculty and administrators from different departments the opportunity to better understand each other, *Looking Ahead* provides schools a chance to learn from each other. Further, *Looking Ahead* shows ways that effective schools link every aspect of school life—the academic program, the admission process, development, athletics and advising systems—through a coherent vision shared by all constituents. *Looking Ahead* will help schools identify what successful programs, policies and systems are in place at other schools and provide the foundation for fruitful discussion groups within each school constituency.

For teachers, *Looking Ahead* will serve as professional development material by profiling innovative academic programs and by providing a clear picture of the faculty's role in external affairs. *Looking Ahead* will suggest ways teachers can work more effectively with their colleagues while retaining their autonomy.

Similarly, administrators will gain a better understanding of how their work relates to that of their colleagues. *Looking Ahead* will propose ways to overcome feelings of isolation and encourage collegiality and cross-pollination.

For parents committee members, trustees, and major donors, *Looking Ahead* will serve to deepen their understanding of independent schools and strengthen their commitment. External constituents will gain a new appreciation of how to be most valuable to the school.

Student leaders too must play an important role in the discussion gen-

1

erated by *Looking Ahead*. Students need to understand the adult culture of their schools. A clearer picture of the issues and the responsibilities of the adult community will help build strong cross-generational lines of communication based on common goals and a shared vocabulary.

While *Looking Ahead* discusses "effective programs" and strategies for implementation, the book is intended as a point of departure for dialogue between schools rather than an end in itself. Since each school possesses unique circumstances and a distinct mission, each will determine what systems are best suited to its particular needs. Thus, the best use of *Looking Ahead* is as the basis for discussion within and between independent school constituencies.

Collectively, independent schools have extraordinary resources for problem solving. We hope this anthology will help each school look at age-old challenges in new ways.

Looking Ahead is meant for educators at all stages in their careers. Whether new to the profession, deciding whether or not to make it a career, or dedicated to private education as a way of life, educators should find the essays herein sparking new ideas to improve the quality of schools.

Patrick F. Bassett &
Louis M. Crosier

Introduction

The Storm in the Midst of Calm: Seven Moral Polarities of Independent Day Schools

by Daniel R. Heischman, Executive Director
Council for Religion in Independent Schools

We independent school people love calm. Among the general population, we are among that small group that would be quite happy spending the day in tranquility with a good book in a quiet place. We love for our classes, our department meetings, our conferences with parents, to go smoothly. Too often we judge the quality of school life by the presence or lack of calm, and I suspect it is fair to say that our personalities are such that if we have the chance, we would avoid conflict at most costs.[1]

At the same time so many of our students need to have models of calmness in their lives, given the sometimes chaotic and unsettled character of the lives they lead, the homes from which they come, the natural inner disquietude which stems from the process of growing up. As Mary Foote tells us, no matter how vocal and "out of control" young people seem to get, they greatly value the presence of adults who go about their work and model their values with calmness.[2] Not only are we predisposed to such calmness, our students (and many of their parents) are searching for it as they look to find their place in an independent day school.

As much as we cherish calmness, and our constituents cherish it in us, school is a place—inevitably, necessarily—of tension. The educational process is one which thrives on the presence of forces which will play off of each other, frequently colliding, and, in the process, hopefully creating

3

an environment for fruitful reflection and growth. Heart and mind, rights and responsibilities, idealism and realism, voices spoken and voices which remain silent, young and old engage in this place of exchange, interplay, and relationship we call the school. In our more optimistic moments, this tension gives life to our work, it is the reason why we are drawn to this peculiar institution; at other times, given our love of calmness, we find this tension vexing, depleting, distracting, challenging to us at the very core of what we value.

As we think about the moral life of this fascinating but potentially draining community, we are prone to expect that a good dose of the ''moral'' in the life of the school will calm things down, settle the conflicts, bring things back under control. Indeed, the moral framework of a common life exists, if for no other reason, to foster order and coherence in a school. Without it, the institution would be, literally and figuratively, chaos. We return to the foundational ideals of our schools, what this educational process is all about in the first place, in order to re-center ourselves and put our difficult work into perspective (and in the process hope that all will be a bit more sanguine and calm). Frustrated by the values we see operating among students or families, confused by the mixed signals we seem to be sending and/or receiving, tired from the hard work of instilling kindness and an atmosphere of mutual respect, we look to a re-injection of the moral into our educational discourse as a means to make life easier, less fragmented, more workable.

What we may not be ready for, however, is the tension which so frequently accompanies a return to our moral roots as institutions. Moral considerations inevitably arise as a result of conflict; their re-emphasis is likely to ease some tensions, yet provoke others. Schools across the country have learned the hard lesson that a return to our basic mission and ideals as a school will not calm the storms; in some cases those storms (and others, as well) are stirred up all the more.

Many school heads will report of experiences when the school decides to take a stand on a particular issue, after much discussion and soul-searching on the part of faculty, administration, and trustees. There is, inevitably, an excitement in the air as the school reasserts, rediscovers itself with renewed moral vigor. Then the crunch comes: a student is expelled for infraction of a new moral code, faculty members turn a blind eye to issues that plead for consistency and unanimity among the adults of the community, various members of the community (young and old alike) grow cynical about the values which the school seems to be promoting. Suddenly it becomes clear to all concerned that this ''moral business'' is something which Liv Ullman once warned us it would be: hard work!

No independent school should plunge into the moral realm, or remind itself that it lives and finds its reason for being in the moral realm, without being aware of some of the difficult polarities contained therein, the hazards that come with the territory, the threat it can be to our yearning for calm. Some of these polarities are familiar, time-honored components of the school world; as much as we like to think otherwise, we have lived with them for generations. Others, however, have surfaced as a result of the unique and challenging times in which we live, and stem from the enormous changes our culture has experienced in recent years.

While the moral polarities of school life do not simply fit into seven categories (albeit a morally and spiritually significant number!), I would like to offer that many as a springboard for a school considering its own moral life and mission in this day and age, as well as some of the other inherent tensions that come with the territory, threatening as they may be to the calm.

* * * * * * * * * *

1. *The polarity between adult and child/youth.* At first glance, this tension seems obvious, reflective of the basic nature of the school being a place where young and old interact. However, as our culture places such a high priority on the meeting of people's needs (and our independent schools certainly reflect that priority), it is instructive to cast a contemporary light on this age-old polarity.

At Generic Country Day School, the faculty morale is low. It is a veteran faculty which prides itself on high academic standards and revels in teaching highly motivated and gifted students. Yet there is widespread concern among this group that the intellectual calibre of student that attends the school is falling; more and more young people that come through its doors have special needs, and the counseling staff (a group of people many of the members of the faculty greet with some skepticism) talk frequently to teachers about the heavy issues and the difficult decisions that face students at school and at home. "Do they want us to be psychological experts as well as science experts?" asks one confused teacher. "Why aren't these things being taken care of at (students') home?" asks another.

While the counseling staff emphasizes the need for students' self-esteem, the identity and self-esteem of the faculty, built around its standards and view of itself as a substantive intellectual community, has been overlooked. Generic Country Day, like so many other schools, must not only reflect on student needs, but the needs of the adults, who come to the institution searching for an identity, a home. An independent school, mindful of its need to build community, must be attentive to the adults seeking to find themselves in this place, alongside of the children and youth engaged in that process. As Garrett Keizer reminds us, how often, in the process of showing the way to students, are we not also, as teachers, groping for the way ourselves?[3]

2. *The polarity between particularity and uniformity.* In the book, *Habits of the Heart*, Robert Bellah and his associates pointed out a curious but telling trait of societies experiencing an intensified emphasis on and expression of individualism: they exhibit more, not less uniformity.[4] Set a group of individuals free to be themselves, and there is a surprising gravitation toward the commonly accepted in its many forms. Freedom from community norms and behavior does not automatically issue in a freedom for new norms.

It is the weekend that many at Generic Country Day had long anticipated: the annual trustee retreat, where members of the Board were being joined by key faculty, parents, alumni/ae as they engaged in a long-range planning session. On Sunday morning, a couple of trustees were looking over the many pages of newsprint which covered the walls of the conference center where the group had been meeting now for a day and a half. One of the trustees was shaking his head, and the other turned to him and asked what he was thinking. ''All of this work,'' he explained as he took a sip from his coffee cup, ''and all of it sounds just like what was said about the other two schools where I have been a trustee. I don't see anything here which says anything unique about Generic.''

Such is the case with many schools, today. In our efforts to be special institutions, we tend to gravitate toward phrases and images which find widespread acceptance or commonly understood meanings. We have a tendency to feel uncomfortable about those things that are particular to, even eccentric about, our institution, perhaps seeing them as drawbacks in our efforts to secure widespread interest in our school. A school that seriously considers its moral mission must be thinking about that which is particular, indeed wonderfully peculiar about it as a community, and not simply resort to what are quickly becoming uniform ways of describing and thinking about itself. The risk inherent in being ourselves, being particular, is the risk we take whenever we are bold enough to stand for what we feel is right: will others follow us, believe in us, buy into our conviction?

3. *The polarity between marketing and introspection.* Our independent schools are under intensive pressure, these days, to engage in aggressive efforts to market, to be known by the general public and be seen in a favorable light throughout the general marketplace. At any particular instance, in virtually all that we do, the need to promote our school is quickly becoming one of the highest priorities, one of the "core values" of the school. As with so many other segments of society, we seek a means, an audience through which we can "tell our story," a story which is, for the most part, laudatory in its depiction of the school.

As important as this need to market can be, to a school, there is an inherent danger to it all: we can easily, even unconsciously, grow to sidestep, overlook, be wary of any form of self-criticism or introspection that detracts from a positive image of the school. The community's self-critical capacity can thus be jeopardized in the process of attempting to look good to the outside world.

The administrative staff at Generic Country Day feels at a deadlock: the head of school has informed the staff that one of the teachers in the upper school, who, in an assembly that dealt with issues of sexual orientation had come out to the school community as a lesbian, has asked him if it would be permissible for her to speak with a reporter at the local newspaper about the event. In her assembly speech she spoke movingly of what it was like to be a lesbian in a community where there was widespread prejudice, and she, no doubt, would be asked to share some of those experiences in the interview with the reporter. Most of the administrators, supportive of the action of the teacher and encouraging of the school community being a more inclusive environment, had no problem with the request. The admission director and development director, however, were worried: what would this represent to the general public, to families interested in sending their children to the school, to conservative alumni/ae who might object to such a proclamation of a teacher's sexual orientation and thus withhold potential contributions from the school (especially at this particular time, when the school was involved in a major capital campaign)? "You know how quickly reputations develop, and how slowly they are shed," the development director warned the group. "It sounds to me as if you feel this place should not be so inclusive, let alone honest," one of the administrators replied.

Like so many institutions, who we really are as a school is quite different from what we might wish to promote. One of the moral tensions which characterize our schools today is the balancing of a healthy, honest understanding of the true nature of our school, including a confrontation with all that is really there, with what we would like to present to the outside world.

4. *The polarity between the school's cultural beginnings and its present inclusivity.* Like many independent day schools, Generic was founded as a non-sectarian institution, but had its cultural underpinnings in a white, Anglo-Saxon, Protestant environment. While there was no creedal uniformity to the school, for many decades the families who attended the institution went to the same churches, recreated at the same country clubs, summered at the same communities. The values of Generic Country Day were implicitly, culturally Christian, although religion was rarely mentioned within the walls of the school (perhaps it did not need to be mentioned, given the implicit agreement).

Two years ago the head of the school met with a group of parents that were concerned about one of the cherished traditions of the school, its Christmas pageant. Muslim, Jewish, and Christian parents alike raised the question, with the head of school, regarding the appropriateness of this assembly—commonly held right before the beginning of the winter holiday—given the fact that the school was, increasingly, a religiously diverse place. Generic Country Day seemed to be sending a message to its students that Christianity was the most important religion, that Christmas was the most important religious holiday, even though the school took no official stand on sectarian belief. They asked the head of school to consider doing away with the pageant. After careful consideration, the head of school made a decision: the event known as the Christmas pageant would no longer be titled as such, the main focus of the assembly would no longer be a re-enactment of the nativity. Instead, a variety of religions and their holidays would be highlighted.

Among faculty and parents, there was both relief and objection. "Finally, I think I can feel included in this place during the month of December," commented one parent. "This school was founded by Presbyterians, and the Christmas pageant has always been a part of the life of the school," argued one faculty member. One of her colleagues on the faculty responded by saying, "But this is a non-sectarian school; religion is not supposed to have any place in this institution." One parent moaned that the "winter festival," as it was now to be called, would have no substance to it, and would be a blend of meaningless, commercial images and allusions.

Be it the school's socioeconomic underpinnings, its implicit religious roots (even though it may be non-sectarian), the independent school of today needs to understand its beginnings, and how that differs from its present-day mission. All too frequently, those differences go unspoken, assumed rather than explicit, and can lie at the heart of why a school feels confused about itself. It is not a calming process to go through, to look at a school's roots and the influence those roots have on the present-day life of the school, but it may be a necessary process as a school strives for a common moral ground in a changed environment.

5. *The polarity between school as a meeting place and school as a launching pad.* Again, drawing upon the insights of Robert Bellah, in his book, *The Good Society*, our contemporary society is characterized by a minimal reliance upon institutions, and then only for the meeting of individual needs.[5] For a great many independent school families, the school is one of the few institutions that they identify with, happily or unhappily, if for no other reason than the fact that this institution will presumably, in the long run, serve to facilitate the individual need for success and advancement as one moves into adulthood. The school becomes a stepping stone, a vehicle for success, viewed less in terms of its inherent value as a place of learning and more in terms of where it can, ultimately, deliver its students.

Such a view of school, of course, collides with the perspective of school being a meeting place, a locus of value and dialogue on what is important to a community, an environment where learning is valued for its own sake and the exchange of ideas and experiences creates a model for what all of life should be like.

It is springtime at Generic Country Day. Many seniors are busy with preparation for Advance Placement Exams, yet there seem to be a variety of problems emerging with the morale and behavior of the senior class. Teachers complain about senior attitudes, their unwillingness to work, their disruptive behavior in assemblies and on senior prank day. The school counselors caution teachers that they are seeing adolescent symptoms of loss and mourning, as these seniors come to terms with leaving the school. Moreover, now that most of them have been accepted into college, it is the first time in their student careers that they have not been "under the gun," absent the threat of college admissions guiding so much of their study and behavior.

The dean of students and class advisors decided that the seniors needed a series of forums, carried out within the confines of the advisory groups, to talk about issues related to leaving Generic and making the transition to college. When the forums were announced, along with the indication that class time would be taken up with these discussions, a number of the AP teachers complained at how their schedules would be disrupted and how there would be no time to complete the syllabus. "We're in danger of compromising our fine AP record," explained one department head. After two long faculty meetings, the head of school reversed the decision, citing the need for a full allotment of time to be given over for AP exam preparation.

Is school a place where the primary task is working out the issues of the community, or is it, above all, a context where individual advancement and achievement are promoted? In most institutions, I think it is fair to say, there is a tendency to live in tandem with these two perspectives. Being one of the few institutions many families affiliate with, there will be increasing pressure on the school to be a meeting ground for many community needs, all of the while still remaining the channel for what lies ahead. Much of the creativity and vitality of a school results from the tension created by these two forces, two values at work, one with the other.

6. *The polarity between school being a safe haven from and school being a mirror of society.* A subtle shift has taken place in many of our schools, as they view themselves and seek better to understand themselves: the independent school has moved significantly from being a place apart to being a place more reflective of the character and makeup of society in general. We seek more to be mirrors of the culture, as opposed to havens from it. On a very positive level, we actively seek to make our student bodies and faculties reflect the growing diversity of our country. On a more reluctant level, we slowly are realizing that certain societal issues cannot be kept out of school, that, to use an image which Paula Lawrence Wehmiller uses, our students cannot check parts of their lives, conditions they encounter in society, at the door when they come to school.[6] As with most subtle shifts, however, there are inherent tensions in that movement, and no small amount of hesitation as to what it means.

One of the second grade teachers at Generic seemed in shock as she spoke with the director of the lower school. "I can't believe it," she explained, "all of a sudden my young children were asking questions about AIDS. I didn't know what to say!" The two of them had a long discussion on the appropriateness of talking about the disease with young children, culminating in a decision, after some days of reflection, to address some of the young students' questions in science class.

Not surprisingly, the lower school director received a call from one parent the evening after the first in a series of science lessons. The parent voiced a strong protest, based on religious grounds, that such topics were being addressed at school. "If I wanted my child to be exposed to such things," she contended, "I would have enrolled him in a public school where they give out condoms." As a frustrating conversation concluded, over the telephone, the lower school director thought about the complications inherent in addressing difficult societal issues in the life of the school.

Many teachers are indeed in shock, in our schools, regarding the issues which students bring with them into school. As there are fewer opportunities in which families address some of these issues, and for many of our students there is no other institution in their lives dedicated to healthy dialogue, the school becomes the focus of complex, often delicate moral issues which overwhelm our society, not to mention our schools.

As one parent concluded, in his conversation with the upper school director, following suspension of his son from school for being an accessory to a cheating incident (the first such punishment as a result of the newly-instituted honor system at Generic Country Day), "I'm not so sure I want my son to be in a place where they have an honor system; I want him to be in a place where they are preparing him for the real world, and cheating is very much a part of that real world. He'll have to deal with it, so he might as well know the ropes right now." An equally frustrating conversation as the one which his lower school colleague experienced, it nonetheless caused him to think about the way in which we prepare young people for the future: is it best to be a place where ideals are valued (and thereby becomes a place different from the norm in society), or should we be more reflective of "what's out there?" If there are differences in what we wish to reflect and what we don't wish to reflect, what are the values implicit behind what we would wish to regard as the "moral mirror"?

7. *The polarity between community responsibility and individual virtue.* Mirroring many of the manifold social issues which our culture faces, the school must often wrestle with the tension inherent in the question, "What's more important?" in a given situation: a larger social issue or the ethics of personal character and virtue? To my mind, this is one of the great dilemmas our schools face today—explicitly or implicitly—when our calmness is disturbed.

Perhaps no greater tension gripped Generic Country Day than the one which existed for several months between the Christian Fellowship on campus and the Cultural Diversity Club. The latter, which included students from a variety of non-Christian backgrounds, had become concerned by the efforts of the Christian Fellowship to evangelize in the school (efforts which had seemed to intensify following the change in the tradition of the Christmas pageant). The Cultural Diversity Club announced in student assembly that it was offended by the "recruiting" techniques of the Christian Fellowship, and called upon the school to set strict guidelines for the control of voluntary religious groups in the school. As that announcement was being made, a number of students involved in the Christian Fellowship walked out of assembly.

The following week, in student assembly, the Christian Fellowship issued a rebuttal, claiming that the Cultural Diversity Club's demand was an infringement on its (the Fellowship's) right to free speech and expression of itself as a Christian group. As the announcement was being made, members of the Cultural Diversity Club, in turn, walked out in protest.

The head of the upper school sat in the midst of a meeting of officers of both clubs, a meeting characterized by charges and counter-charges regarding issues of free speech and respect for differences. "I think we're missing something here," the upper school head remarked in an effort to restore some civility to the discourse. "All of you are talking about your rights as a group and your demand to be respected for those rights, but no one seems to notice how you are treating each other."

Christina Hoff Sommers has argued that our society is characterized by a "silence about virtue,"[7], a reluctance to consider the dimension of individual character as we think through, argue about moral issues on the corporate level. That leaves us with almost a single-minded focus on ideology and institutional policy, and, accordingly, ". . . the student loses sight of himself (or herself) as a moral agent and begins to see himself (or herself) as a moral spectator or protojurist." [8]. Much of what we must do, in our schools as we address the community implications of larger social and institutional issues, has to do with emphasizing the daily, individual, implications of our moral concern, seen in how we take responsibility for our own actions and how we treat each other in the process, trivial as it may seem in the face of the larger, wide-ranging problems.

* * * * * * * * * *

In a recent discussion on the role of a school head in making moral decisions, Fran Norris Scoble concluded, "Most moral decisions fall into the gray area; I would welcome a little, clean-cut, good vs. evil in my life as a school head."[9] The calmness we naturally seek, the moral consensus we yearn for, may eventually come, indeed may be the possession of some schools already. For most independent day schools, however, the task remains one that is difficult and, at times, disturbing, the result of our own making as well as that we inherit from forces beyond our control. It is vexing work, something we might have hoped the "moral" would save us from, rather than force us to face. That does not make the task any less important, the search for a truth both deeply personal and community-wide any less essential. In the words of a famous educator, "You cannot be a zero . . . and be a seeker after truth. The very search makes you something." [10] As much as we cherish the calm, we are made better, even more clearly defined, by the storms!

NOTES

1. Parker Palmer frequently speaks of the role to which educators gravitate in downplaying or avoiding conflict; likewise, in a recent book, *Meeting at the Crossroads: Women's Psychology and Girls' Development* (Harvard University Press, 1992), Lyn Mikel Brown and Carol Gilligan address the frequency with which female students and their teachers silence themselves for fear of conflict.

2. Taken from a talk by Mary Foote, "Values and Families: A Close Relationship," given to the parents of Horace Mann School (NY) in the winter of 1993.

3. Garrett Keizer, *No Place But Here* (Penguin Books, 1989), p. 164.

4. See Robert Bellah and others, *Habits of the Heart* (Harper & Row, 1985), pp. 142–163.

5. See Robert Bellah, *The Good Society* (Alfred A. Knopf, 1991).

6. See Paula Wehmiller, *Face to Face: Lessons Learned on the Teaching Journey* (Friends Council on Education, 1992).

7. Christina Hoff Sommers, "Ethics Without Virtue: Moral Education in America," *American Scholar* 53:381–389 (1984).

8. Ibid., p. 388.

9. Taken from a NAIS session, "The Moral Dimensions of Headship," San Francisco, CA, 1992.

10. Howard Foster Lowry, *College Talks* (Oxford University Press, 1969), p. 53.

1

The Face of Education in the Future

by Patrick F. Bassett, President
Independent Schools Association of the Central States

I walk through the long schoolroom questioning
A kind old nun in a white hood replies;
The children learn to cipher and to sing,
To study reading-books and history,
To cut and sew, be neat in everything
In the best modern way. . . .
—William Butler Yeats, "Among School Children"

I have seen the face of education in the future: it is bright-eyed, digitized, on-line, and up and operating at The New Laboratory for Teaching and Learning at The Dalton School, a progressive independent day school in New York City. Spearheaded by a $2 million grant from a school patron, invigorated by a collaboration between the school and Columbia's Teachers College, and directed by a visionary iconoclast, Frank Moretti, classes have begun at the school of the future.

Enter a New Lab sixth grade social studies class, and you will see the basic configuration of the classroom for tomorrow (if there is to be such a quaint architectural anachronism as a classroom in the future): four computers on-line and networked with the centralized server of the school, with "teams" of student-workers collaborating on their component of the project of the moment. In this case, the group is exploring ArcheoType, a Dalton Technology Plan New Lab program created by the Dalton staff, including Mary Kate Brown, resident archaeologist, and Neil Goldberg (whose technical genius and imagination in creating the program suggests he is related to another Goldberg renowned for unusual

15

creations, Rube). ArcheoType is a program that simulates the actual experience of an archaeologist working on an ancient Assyrian site. Given the extraordinary graphical possibilities now available via Apple's Hypercard for Macintosh (and comparable technologies for PCs in Windows), teachers can now create the most amazing simulations, ones that create an environment so rich and realistic that literally the boundaries of classroom and school disappear. In the case of ArcheoType, for example, the students' computers reveal an archaeological excavation site divided into a grid; each team chooses one grid area and then starts sifting with a "screen": we actually see the screen sifting and hear the sounds of an archaeologist at work as dirt filters through the screen ("shus-shus-shus"), and we capture the thrill of discovery as one group begins to uncover its first artifact. In this case the students uncover a bas-relief revealing a lion hunt: they then literally "move" the artifact (via mouse) to the laboratory on screen, where they weigh it, measure it, and begin making observation notes about it. Since the bas-relief shows the hunters in a chariot, the students recognize that the style of the chariot, especially the number of spokes in the wheel, may place the chariot and thus the bas-relief within a specific historical period. The next step in the process of discovery, then, is to compare this chariot image with others, cataloged on line from artifact images scanned into the school's server database from various library and museum sources. Once a match has been made, inductive hypotheses begin to form. Since the teachers themselves have created this excavation site, they made it perhaps the richest collection of Assyrian artifacts yet discovered, but not without some red herrings: a vase from an itinerant Roman mixed into one grid throws one group off track: not to fear, since all groups have access to the research notes by other groups, so that eventually each team learns from the work and discoveries of others. Since some of the students have computers with modems at home, it is possible for them to call into the school computer anytime: in fact, this facility is the source of backlog and backup, since so many students wish to keep working well beyond school hours and bedtime for that matter. Some of the sixth graders follow their teachers into the bathroom, not wishing to lose the train of thought they are currently exploring because of some extraneous distraction, like the bell for the next class. Although the final project for the unit is a traditional research paper (Don't all sixth graders write comprehensive scientific research papers?), the experience of producing the final exhibition has been exhilarating for students and teacher. So much for passive learning, teacher as lecturer, classroom-bound and textbook-bound education (the bane of traditional, modern schools of the Industrial Age). Some applause, please, for the post-modern, Information Age school of the future.

Walk around the corner to an English class led by department chair Steven Bender and English teacher Jacqueline D'Aiutoio to enter into the new world of teaching Shakespeare. As a former English teacher myself, it is safe for me to say that it is the rare pedagogue who enjoys teaching Shakespeare to adolescents. Now we may sublimate and project a bit because those of us who know the Bard like him and admire his wit, but trying to guide adolescents through a text of words and ideas that are remote at best to creatures whose own language and argot is obscure is no picnic. So give me a sonnet to teach, or *Catcher in the Rye*, but please not the albatross of *Macbeth*. Unless, of course, I had the resources of the New Lab at Dalton School and could work with Teachers College professor Robert McClintock in creating Playbill. In that case, I might overcome the inherent skepticism of all English teachers that the computer can invigorate the literary text itself, sort of what happened to Steve Bender and Jackie D'Aiutoio, initially skeptics themselves. Open Playbill to *Macbeth*, and you find a world to explore that few Shakespeare scholars themselves have the time and resources to exhaust. Herein lies the full text, any and all critical expositions on the text that the teacher and students find readable and germane. Rather than assign the teacher's favorite topics, the program encourages students to identify interests and make explorations on their own, in fact to scan into the database the critical essays which they, not the teacher, find illuminating. A colleague walks into the class, and exclaims, "Well, *Macbeth* is the most sanguinary of plays," but a student challenges that: "Let's do a search." His search for the words *bloody* and *blood* reveal only a handful of references, and exploration of them in context shows only a modicum of bloodthirsty proclivities in the play, at least less than the teacher, now properly chastised, has asserted. Mr. Bender himself wonders about the purpose of the porter scene, so he and the class begin exploring. Since they have three versions of *Macbeth* on CD-ROM disk, they can digitize the porter scenes from all three film versions and place the scenes in the Playbill file; hit a couple of buttons to play all three scenes on the screen, and freeze them there all at once. Gee, it is interesting that the Polanski treatment is different from the Orson Wells treatment, which is different yet from the BBC version. Well, maybe we can learn from the actual staging of the scene what the possibilities of the meaning of the scene may be. . . . And so it goes with teaching and learning about *Macbeth* in the school of tomorrow. It's so much fun, maybe we'll take the class to the Joseph Papp

production of Shakespeare in the Park. Can't get away from note cards
and three-part essays? That's OK, since the note cards and papers the
students write are embedded into the program itself, so all students can
read and comment upon each other's thinking and work. Sounds a lot like
what Ted Sizer (Brown University and founding force behind the Coali-
tion of Essential Schools) and Mortimer Adler (philosopher and architect
of Paedeia Proposal Schools) have been talking about in terms of group
work, collaborative learning, teacher as coach, and projects as demonstrations of learning, right?

Think this stuff is only bells and whistles for the creative humanists in
the faculty? Guess again by going to an astronomy class led by the
ebullient and witty Malcolm Thompson, Dalton science department
teacher and holder of the Thompson Chair in Science. His Project Galileo
develops from the considerable resources available in the public and
commercial domains, developed initially for the serious amateur astron-
omer. Under Malcolm's tutelage and inspired by the innate curiosity of
his budding scientist students, Project Galileo has evolved in some seriously impressive directions. Like to see a portion of the sky at any point
from 5000 BC to 5000 AD? No problem for Project Galileo. Like to see
it from the vantage point of Mars rather than from Earth? We can transport you there electronically in a flash that Flash Gordon might envy. I
wonder what the last eclipse looked like from various points along the
Pacific coastline of the Americas. . . . (I can see it, actually, in simulated
form, as one student's animated version of the eclipse demonstrates.)
How about hooking into the largest telescope in America, Mount Wilson?
No problem, since we are online through our modem and since Mount
Wilson, publicly owned, allows us occasionally to train its telescope
wherever we want to go. Do you mean that high school students are doing
real science? Yep, as they will in all the schools of tomorrow that we must
create starting today.

What window on the past does the technology of the future provide that
we don't already have in the library? What's a library? Do you mean the
media center? When Luyen Chou (Dalton School grad, philosophy major
and now Associate Director of the The New Laboratory School) and
Thomas de Zengotita (Co-director of the Tishman Project) envisioned
History Maker, they had in mind the historiographical notion of history,
that sophisticated students of history research the point of view of the
observer as much as the observed events in trying to ascertain what
happened and why it happened. And so it goes as the eleventh grade Civil
War Project in the Dalton School focused on the New York City draft

riots of 1863. The students did go to the library, both the school library and the New York Public Library, to find historical photographs of the Brooks Brother block (center of the riots), scanned them into the database, then scanned in as well their own photographs of current buildings on the block for purposes of comparison and contrast. The class went on a three-hour walking tour with peripatetic Professor of History at Columbia College James Shenton, whom they videotaped, digitized, and added to the database to call up onto a portion of the screen as one of the many resources for some of the term papers produced. Oh, by the way, forget killing trees, anymore, since the students write, edit, and submit their term papers on-line. Going to sleep at the thought of reading 90 sophomore (and too often sophomoric) term papers? Hold onto your mouse, since reading these papers is a ride on the wild side. Come to a boldfaced phrase of the student's text, click on it, and one of the primary documents referred to at that moment in the text appears (e.g., The 1863 *New York Times* front page article on the riots). Scan down to a boxed word in the next paper, click on it, and low and behold, there is a segment of the professor's lecture from the street corner. As an African-American student, are you disturbed since there is nothing in the traditional texts about your ancestors' part in and reaction to these riots? Well, this is History Maker, after all, so let's do just that: interview descendants, find diaries, scan photographs of the African-American diarists into the program and then ask your gifted friends to do a dramatic reading of the passage. Yikes: this is starting to put Ken Burns' *Civil War* documentary to shame. What about using a photograph in your paper/project that dramatizes your point (bones from a mass grave) but that actually comes from another time and event altogether? Maybe, maybe not: but you'll have to face the wrath of some of the other class members who argue vociferously that such a strategy is not history at all, but propaganda. You mean kids are fighting over each others' history papers? Lots of good stuff here as we look back from the school of tomorrow.

Any traditionalists in the crowd who object to the new technology and the new pedagogy upon which it is based tend to do so on the grounds of their own rich experience with texts, their love of the physical properties of words, and their fear that the very humanity of discourse will be lost in the brave new world of technology-based instruction. In fact, it is often the most articulate and flamboyant of classroom dramatists who, unsurprisingly, are the most vehement resistors to computerization of the curriculum. Somehow, they see themselves as Socrates with so many budding Platos at their feet, and they consequently remain unwilling to

sacrifice the honor and chemistry of that paradigm for what they consider
to be mere "appliances." This is where Frank Moretti steps up to parry
the slings and arrows of outrageous opposition. In careful didactic and
rather traditional manner, Dr. Moretti presents to academicians the historical overview of the educational and cultural transformation he sees
transpiring by documenting and assessing the very nature of three epochs:
the onset of the literary age (supplanting the ancient Oral Tradition world
of the Classicists) propelled by the invention of the alphabet; the onset of
the Modern Age of the Gutenberg Revolution embodied educationally in
the development of the printed text; the onset of the Information Age of
the Post-modern Revolution produced as the result of the new computer
technology of digital storage and transmittal of information. Each tech-
nological advancement represented in this progression has been accompanied by a paradigm shift in education.

Before the invention of the alphabet (5th century B.C.), the Agrarian
Age was educationally based on an oral tradition. The world was understood through the passing on orally of epic stories which lionized heroic
figures: Abraham and Moses; Achilles and Odysseus; etc. Stories were
constructed in recitable and paradigmatic forms, and storytellers were
trained to pass on the stories from generation to generation, the Homeric
oral tradition being the apex of its manifestation. Around the 5th century
B.C., however, one of the universe's most significant inventions, the
alphabet, transformed learning and thereby education. We became a lit-
eracy-based civilization, and knowledge itself was transformed. The
Socratic dialogue was the pedagogic model: Socrates tutoring Plato, who
mentored Aristotle, who in turn was the tutor of Alexander the Great. In
the Aristotelian world, one posited a division between knowledge (philosophy and theology) and power (rhetoric), the tension between them
being both political (Socrates' death at the hands of the state and Galileo's
excommunication by the Church roughly marking both ends of this epoch) and philosophical. Moretti argues it is in this epoch that the idea of
the soul was invented, clearly the focus of much of the search for knowledge of the age.

Moretti asserts that it is Gutenberg's press and the resulting proliferation of the printed text that is the marker of the next transformational
revolution in knowledge and education. It is the development of the
printed text that made possible the modern school, with students collected
in a classroom and led by a scholar/professor who helps them to read and
understand a text, the basic model of schooling that has been unchanged
from the 16th century until the present. The specialization and division of

labors became incarnate in education in the form of distinctive bodies of knowledge, specific disciplines, and the divisions of education that still dominate the way in which we structure knowledge and organize schools and that incidentally foreshadowed a parallel division and specialization of labors of the factory model of the Industrial Age that followed. Like the assembly line, the student path is convergent and centripetal, a basically reductionist process in which the teacher interprets and reduces the text for classroom lecture and the student further reduces that information into "what one needs to know to pass the test." Like the marketplace, the motivation and assessment of success is based on a competitive model. The role of the teacher is to dramatize and illuminate the known, that which is to the young to some extent or another incomprehensibly encoded within the text. Space and time in the modern school since the 16th century have not changed: we operate by divisions into tangible units of classrooms and periods. The culture of schools became one of constraint: to conventionalize and standardize young people so that they shared a common body of knowledge and a common value system to support and perpetuate the culture through social control and instruction that encouraged passive receipt of approved knowledge.

Listening to Moretti, one cannot help remembering the flippant remark made by George Bernard Shaw regarding his schooling: "The only time my education was interrupted was when I was in school." Moretti posits, the New Lab at Dalton School manifests, and I believe that the onset of computerization and the Information Age will usher in the epoch of the post-modern school, transforming the art, the architecture, the pedagogy, and the means of the education of our youth. Unlike the current model, the post-modern school will be a product of and contributor to The Information Age. The student path will be divergent and centrifugal: learning will be problem-solving oriented and teaching will be resource-based, the teacher functioning more as coach and guide to the information and resources available in a global network. The basic task of schooling will be to teach the student how to penetrate the global network of data and information available and growing at geometric rates, how to assess, assimilate, and synthesize that information, and how to recast it in meaningful ways to solve the problem of the moment. Motivation and assessment will also shift, the primary impulse propelling learning being the need to work collaboratively in the task force assigned to the problem, one's work then becoming part of individual and collective portfolios demonstrating mastery of the skills involved. Unless the new models of work in the marketplace shift away from what we are now seeing (quality circles, total quality management and like concepts that emphasize collaborative problem-solving), this new approach in the schools will have a smoother and more direct relationship to skills necessary for success in the workplace than our current models (in which, if business is to be believed, there is little carryover, and that which does exist is often counterproductive). The teacher's role has shifted dramatically, as well, from that of the showman to that of the strategist, the navigator of the unpredictable. Space and time will become liberated: just as AT&T now permits a percentage of its workers to work outside the corporate setting via computer modem and network, so too will schools begin to adopt more flexibility in their definition of workplace and school time. Space and time will be up for grabs. Want to plan the new campus of the future? Focus on the gym, since it may be the only physical facility on the premises. Finally, in the post-modern world of the Information Age, the very concept of school will shift from the place where conforming constraints are both the observable and hidden curriculum to where individual inquiry, discovery, and development are manifest.

On the pages of educational journals and within the popular media, the debates will continue to rage over the issues of the modern school in its current manifestation. We will argue about reforms and restructuring (longer school days and school years, site-based management, etc.); we will debate school choice (public support of private school options); we will fight over curriculum (multiculturalism vs. the canon); we will clash over testing (standardized vs. portfolio demonstrations). All of these conundrums are the dying gasps of the modern school, since all will disappear in the post-modern school of the Information Age. The new schools will transcend each of these issues with the new approaches embodied and encoded within the new technology and the limitless opportunities made available through it. For a nation founded on the possibilities inherent in unfettered freedom and one propelled into world leadership because of the combined power of imagination and resources, the new school of the Information Age will be our greatest achievement for it will liberate and empower all children, not just the fortunate few who attend prosperous schools. The New Lab at Dalton School is showing us the way: the rest of us need to follow.

2

Community Service

by Linda Anderson, Community Service Coordinator
The Potomac School

Community service is an increasingly important component in the total educational program of the contemporary independent school. Over the last decade there has been a marked growth in the number of independent schools involved in these programs, and the programs themselves have become more complex and sophisticated. This is also true of public schools, with at least one state making community service a requirement for graduation. There are some very good reasons for this trend. Educators have come to appreciate the value of community service in achieving the overarching goals of developing the students' potential as responsible citizens and providing them with an education that transcends the confines of the classroom and the sports field. Specifically, these programs are seen as means of broadening the students' understanding of people, especially those not so privileged, and students' awareness of society's many problems and challenges. In contributing their efforts, they will not only gain this understanding, but realize that they can make a positive difference in the lives of others. The intended result of these experiences is the growth and development of the students' character and personal qualities and their abilities to relate to and work with others. A successful program will nurture lifelong habits of service and cultivate volunteerism as a spontaneous and normal part of community living.

Perhaps another aspect of this trend in instituting service programs is that educational institutions are accepting more, and are expected to accept more, responsibility for instilling moral and ethical values in their students, as other societal institutions find their roles diminished. A community service program not only fits in very comfortably with these efforts but can be an essential part of them. Even schools with existing service programs are reevaluating, updating and revising their programs in light of these new expectations.

Admittedly, service programs also have their symbolic value. It would be rare to find the head of a school who is oblivious to the public image of his institution. A visible service program can undoubtedly help foster a positive public image, especially for an independent school that some might view as a sheltered enclave for the wealthy. Such symbolic value cannot be ignored, but must be carefully considered and contained. Symbol without substance can lead to the opposite results of those discussed above, with students gaining a superficial view of their world and a cynical regard for those who run it. Students should receive recognition for their efforts but that recognition must be deserved.

Historically, the earliest service programs were developed in schools with religious affiliations. In the Quaker Friend's schools and Catholic Jesuit and Sacred Heart schools, as prominent examples, service was and is an integral part of the institutions' fundamental philosophy and mission. When parents and children considered and chose these schools, it was very clear that service would be a significant part of the educational process. There was a similar understanding on the part of faculty and administrators choosing to work in these institutions. Other schools developed service programs out of the growing conviction of their importance and to offer a new, less traditional approach to learning. In both of these types of programs time is often allotted in the weekly academic schedule for service, thus imparting a strong institutional validation to its existence and value. Schools with such historical backgrounds and philosophical mandates provide much from which other schools may draw; however, they cannot be taken simply as models to imitate. Although it is essential to review and study other schools' service programs, each school has its own distinctive educational philosophy and personality, and its service program must be fully compatible with its distinctive character. Also, among the more practical variables to be considered are the school's location, size, budget, service opportunities, and parental and faculty commitment. Each school then must custom design a program to suit itself and its environs. This may be an initially modest program upon which the institution may build over time. Nonetheless, there are certain key elements that appear to bind successful programs together. These elements must be firmly established at the very beginning if a program has much of a chance of surviving.

To begin with, it is vital that the concept of service be incorporated in the mission of the school. Unless it is spelled out in the written philosophy of the school, the faculty or administrators who are responsible for co-ordinating projects will have a difficult time getting others to take them seriously. A service program without such documentary validation will find itself functioning outside of the mainstream of the school. This documentary validation should be the result of a deliberative and educational process in which, ideally, faculty, parents and students are involved. At the end of this process, all those involved will be aware of the significance of the event and that service will henceforth be a part of the fabric of the school's daily life.

The role of the service coordinator as a facilitator, administrator, advocate, and general resource person is obviously important for a service program that is effective and responds to the needs of the students. This person must have energy and enthusiasm and be able to reach out in many directions. Not to be overlooked is the role of the parents. Their understanding and support for the program is also essential. As a practical matter, they will be called on to provide logistical support, such as transportation, financial aid, and resource information. But more importantly, they can provide needed reinforcement and support for their children as they sort through the many aspects of their service experiences. Parents, once they have seen the positive educational and emotional benefits of service, can become very strong advocates for the program.

Once service becomes an integral part of the overall philosophy of the school and a coordinator is selected, then it is necessary to organize a program. Fortunately, there is now a wealth of detailed material readily available to help schools do this. The essential element in this part of the process is that a service program must focus on the developmental needs of the students. If it does so, it probably can't go far wrong. The objective of the service program should not be muddled by secondary reasons for existence. All service opportunities and placements must be carefully selected to remain true to this overall goal. This generally means that projects should be people-oriented and respond to direct human needs. They should largely not be one-time events but continuing activities. This is the essence of a successful program. However, there are many other worthwhile projects that do not respond directly to human needs but can still support the program's objectives. Projects that require students to work together cooperatively, such as a clean-up or a "gleaning," fall into this category.

The coordinator must begin building a catalogue of potential projects and a database of placement opportunities. There are many resources that can be tapped in doing this. A survey of the parent and faculty community is a logical starting point and will probably be the best resource. There is nothing like first-hand knowledge from those in the community. Talking with churches and synagogues about agencies and programs that they have found to be good for their youth groups is particularly useful. Contact with other schools and their service coordinators can also of great help. In the Washington D.C. metro area, service coordinators meet bimonthly to share information on successful (and unsuccessful) service opportunities. There may be a local volunteer center that coordinates volunteer activities for all ages on which to draw. Local newspapers often publish announcements, information and highlights about volunteer efforts or agencies in their areas. Most areas will yield an abundance of resources and opportunities. It will be up to the coordinator to explore and evaluate these opportunities and recommend those that will best serve the objectives of the program. Agency and volunteer information changes frequently, so it is important to keep directories and files current.

The implementation of the program should be organized as a three-phase process. The first phase is the preparation phase. As in any educational experience, students need to gain some overall perspective before they can begin their educational journeys. They need to become acquainted with the nature and origins of various service opportunities, the attendant issues and problems, governmental action and policies, and so on. This phase will serve to heighten the students' interest and readiness to serve. A good preparation phase should enable students to choose areas that they believe are important and in which they want to become involved. To place students in service opportunities without proper preparation will detract from both their performances and their gaining from their experiences. It is very helpful during this phase to invite representatives from receiving agencies to talk to the students and answer their questions.

The next phase is the placement of the student in an appropriate service opportunity. After the preparation phase, the service coordinator should be able to determine which service opportunities will work best for each student and why. Also, if the preparation has been effective, the student will be able to define areas of interest. To make a good placement, the coordinator must have firsthand knowledge of receiving agencies in their school area and maintain accurate, current and thorough files of opportunities within each. Ideally, the coordinator will have visited each location and established a rapport with the organizations' leaders. When the coordinator discusses service opportunities with the agency, it is vital to get a clear description of the exact nature of the duties the students will be performing and what the expectations are from the agency. These must be conveyed to the student.

The third phase is the actual performance of service. During this phase the coordinator must maintain continuing contact with both the volunteer and the receiving agency. If the coordinator receives feedback from students or other members of the community (e.g., parents) that the service location is not what it is billed to be, or if they are using students to perform tasks that were not clearly discussed, then the coordinator should review the situation with the agency. If this does not solve the problem, then the listing should be removed from the reference directory. On the other hand, if the coordinator receives feedback from the agency that the students are not adequately performing their duties, then the student should be counseled on his responsibilities. In sum, it is essential that the communications among the agency, the coordinator and the student are always clear and continuous.

The fourth phase in the service process is the individual student's reflection on his or her experiences and a sharing of these reflections with others. This is an essential part of achieving the educational goals of the service program. Practically speaking, this means that each student must write or talk about his experiences. There are many ways of bringing this about: student diaries and journals, written reports (perhaps as a part of an independent study project), small group discussions, oral reports in academic classes or school assemblies. Faculty members should be especially attuned to this phase of the process and its importance. The student's reflection phase rounds out the cycle of a successful learning experience.

There are a number of running issues concerning school service programs. Mandatory versus voluntary is an issue that inescapably comes up. There are very good and valid reasons for both positions. The only valid generalization is that each school must consider its own situation and do what it thinks best for its students. In the best of worlds, all students would participate on a voluntary basis. Seeing the opportunity to do good, all students would naturally respond to the challenge. This does not often happen. Even a well-led program within a generally motivated student population, can fail to elicit the participation of a significant number of students. Some students are truly very busy with other worthwhile activities. Others may be apprehensive about the program for a variety of reasons (e.g., having to work with the elderly, the handicapped, minorities, etc.). Others just don't want to be bothered.

If you believe that some aspects of the service program are sufficiently important so that all students should experience them, even on a compulsory basis, then you will be in good company if you make the program mandatory. As one faculty convert to a mandatory program expressed it, "Perhaps the issue that sealed my conversion was that of the new awareness possible for any student engaging in a service program. Part of that new awareness centered on students awakening to new capacities within themselves, capacities for persistence, tenderness, toughness, dedication, and feeling. In addition students would awaken to perhaps untouched power to make a concrete and significant difference in the life of another person; few revelations can affect the developing mind and heart more than this one."[1] Following on that thought, once immersed, some students will overcome any initial reluctance and be happy to have had the opportunity to serve. Students have been known to endorse mandatory service because they realized that they needed a little push in the right direction. Of less importance, but still of some significance, the phases of the service program, as discussed above, are in many ways easier to implement and control in a mandatory program.

Proponents of all voluntary programs usually emphasize the importance of developing the spirit of volunteerism. This obviously becomes more problematic in a mandatory situation. Unfortunately, the issue of mandatory versus voluntary is often discussed as being a case of either/or. It need not be. A school may establish a mandatory service component to ensure that all students gain at least some important benefits from participation, such as an exposure to problems and conditions about which they would otherwise remain ignorant. Probably, the goal of nurturing a spirit of volunteerism will not be maximized under those circumstances. But that school might also have a thriving voluntary component that will more fully meet all the goals of a school service program, at least for those who participate. Maximizing voluntary participation would still be an objective. In fact, if a school has only a mandatory program, it might well indicate a general lack of commitment to service on the part of the school. Such a program could easily degenerate into an empty symbolic exercise of use to no one.

Another issue that arises in both the mandatory and voluntary context is whether academic credit should be given for service. Arguments can

---

[1] John Grega of the McDonogh School, Baltimore, Maryland, in "The National Community Service Network News," The Council for Religion in Independent Schools, April 1993.

also be made on both sides of this issue. On the one hand, credit can convey the message that participants must "get" something tangible for their efforts. On the other hand, it is a means of officially validating the program. There are clear cases where academic credit is fully justified, at least at the high school level. As an actual example, a successful twenty-year-old voluntary program not only gives credit, but offers community service as a semester course. The preparation phase, as described above, is much more academically oriented, with students doing in-depth reading on the nature of their chosen service assignments, such as early child development or mental illness. Next, the students' work is monitored and evaluated. The students are required to keep daily journals, and write analyses, self-evaluations, personal reflections and a final report on their experiences. In spite of the formality and rigor of such a program, the participation rate is 90%. As it happens, it fits in with the educational philosophy of the Jesuit institution in question. Also, some academic courses can have a service component as a natural adjunct. For example, some courses in civics and American government require students to "volunteer" a certain number of hours in local governmental agencies as a part of the learning process.

As yet another approach, "service learning" is a fairly recent innovation for weaving the concept of community service into a school's culture by incorporating at every school level, and in every course possible, learning activities that are service-related. Thus, the community service thread would run through the entire curriculum. As examples: math problems in the lower school might require students to calculate how many pounds of each vegetable to put in a 50-gallon soup kitchen pot; typing classes might write letters to shut-ins; chemistry classes might monitor the water purity of local rivers and lakes. The possibilities are endless. This concept should be a powerful complement to the more conventional service program. Obviously, a systematic introduction of service learning takes a considerable amount of commitment and effort on the part of the school faculty. Probably for this reason, relatively few schools so far have embraced this methodology. Again, there are materials and seminars available for guiding a school's efforts in installing service learning.

It goes without saying that the development of a successful service program must be age appropriate. In general, lower and middle schools have had success with service projects that revolve around group efforts and projects. A good example of a lower school program is a class field trip to a local nursing home on a continuing basis so that the students can develop relationships with the residents. Other examples could involve work in soup kitchens or environmental projects. Middle schoolers could choose projects that stretch them a bit, such as working with mentally retarded adults in group homes. Often many of these efforts start out as group endeavors, with middle school students taking on individual responsibilities on their own initiative. The keys here are that the students have time to prepare and reflect on their efforts and establish a commitment through consistent visits.

Upper school service programs can run the gamut of short and long-term programs. At this level, developing student leadership also becomes more important. A student service advisory board is a preferred means of generating, structuring and leading projects and programs. There are many possibilities for both group and individual efforts. There can be group projects where students mount one-time efforts to mobilize the entire school community for such activities as food drives, dances for senior citizens, field days for kids from the inner city, river clean-ups and collecting supplies for disaster relief. Individual placement of students can be in weekly or monthly assignments in perhaps a year-long program, such as tutoring, hospital work, or therapeutic riding or swimming. Often these placements require training from the receiving agencies. At times, schools in the same area can join together in multi-school projects, such as a "gleaning."

Community service can and should be an essential part of the educational programs of most if not all of today's independent schools. The entire community should reap the rewards of a successful program for years to come. Successful programs, though, must be based on the individual circumstances of each institution and honor the mission of that school and the developmental needs of its students.

3

The Real World as Classroom

by Elisabeth Griffith, Head of School
The Madeira School

Long before the MS. Foundation's "Take Our Daughters To Work Day," long before President Clinton's call for vocational education and a youth service corps, and long before the Carnegie Council's 1983 recommendation that every high school student be engaged in community service, Madeira School created a unique program to put girls in the work place for "on the job training" in the "real world." Every Wednesday since 1966 every sophomore, junior, and senior commutes to a volunteer internship. Freshmen stay on campus for a full day of activity and adventure. For one-fifth of their academic program, our students grow in competence and gain self-confidence outside their classrooms, in their Co-curriculum.

Madeira's Co-curriculum combines life survival skills, volunteer service, and professional internships. Although they stay on campus, freshmen are not static. Their day encompasses innovative classes, outdoor activity, art, sports, and field trips. In small morning sections, they rotate among four classes: ethics, computer literacy, family life and health (sex ed), and survival skills, broadly defined to encompass note-taking, test and stress strategies, public speaking, ironing, checkbook balancing, baking, car maintenance, and bicycle repair. After lunch comes a variety of art projects (ceramics, paper and book making, design, and bead work), swimming, and Inner Quest, which converts Madeira's 400-acre campus into an Outward Bound course. This "routine" is broken up by field trips to the National Gallery, the Air and Space Museum, the zoo, the Jefferson Memorial at cherry blossom time, the Vietnam Memorial on Veteran's

31

Day, Gettysburg and Williamsburg. The freshman year offers enough
flexibility so that new additions such as self-defense and musical performance can be included. Freshman year ends with a placement fair, at
which students select their sophomore service assignments. Their choices
include child care centers, nursing homes, hospitals, hospices, halfway
houses, horse riding programs for the disabled, public school classrooms,
and ESL programs. Under the aegis of the Urban League, Madeira is in
a partnership with Tyler Elementary School in Washington, D.C. Most
recently Tyler fourth graders spent Earth Day on our campus, engaged in
science and art projects. Sophomores balance their real life experiences
with an ethics seminar and a speaker series, both of which address such
issues as poverty, homelessness, race prejudice, and health care.

Every junior commutes to Capitol Hill. Following an 8 AM public
affairs class taught on campus, girls spend the day working for Senators
or Representatives, frequently from their home districts. Once a month
they meet at noon for a brown bag briefing by politicians, journalists, Hill
staffers, political consultants, pollsters, or Foreign Service officers, who
are often alumnae or parents. A recent seminar topic was sexual harassment and self-defense, given by the Capitol Hill Police. For one week in
March, junior girls in good standing may choose to spend five full working days on the Hill. The girls are expected to complete a legislative
position paper and keep a journal of their observations.

For their senior year placements, girls have an opportunity to explore
future careers. Many return to social service agencies. Others choose
internships in news agencies, investment houses, research labs, museums
and businesses. One student created an art program for patients in the
burn unit at Children's Hospital; another researched an exhibition catalogue for the Corcoran Gallery. Another student conducted parasitology
research at the National Institutes of Health; another studied turtles at the
Smithsonian. An intern at CBS Evening News found the slide she needed
to illustrate a story on the Persian Gulf War in Madeira's art history
collection. At National Public Radio and Voice of America bilingual
students were on-the-air translators for foreign correspondents. After ar-
chitects designed a new library and sports center for Madeira, a senior
made the cardboard models. A thespian assisted at the Folger Shakespeare
Theater. Folk wisdom on campus is that some girls decide NOT to become veterinarians after a year on the job. Throughout the year seniors
meet formally and informally with alumnae to discuss future options.

In the jargon of "outcome-based education," the Co-curriculum produces tangible results. Now that the Co-curriculum program is 26 years

old, many alumnae recall how their senior placements became resumé entries and helped them get a job after college—both by providing real skills and by proving that they had workplace experience. Learning to be an effective and professional volunteer and meeting a supervisor's expectations outside the classroom reinforce traditional school values. It also gives a student who may be an average student academically an alternate route to achievement. Learning standard office skills from answering phones to filing to entering data is useful, as is a sense of worker reality—of office dress codes, commuting, lunch hours, and the pace and pulse of office life. Those who find it boring have new appreciation for the kinds of work women do. Other outcomes include having a subject for a college essay or another letter of recommendation.

Learning to be an adult in an environment in which co-workers not only allow you to call them by first names but hold you accountable for your performance is another way we help students grow up. Becoming competent, confident and connected is especially important for young women today. The message that ''you can do anything'' is tested weekly in our Co-curriculum. The expanded variety of role models and mentors girls meet and observe reiterates the message. (A note on role models: It is unlikely that despite steadfast efforts, Madeira's adult population will soon reflect the diversity of its student body, 38% of whom are young women of color from 30 states and 30 countries. Among Co-curriculum supervisors girls meet many women to emulate.)

Two unexpected outcomes of the Co-curriculum relate to current social trends. The contributions Madeira students make to our surrounding community, whether measured in hours or empathy, provide some insurance for the institution were we ever challenged to justify our tax-exempt status. On a long list of ways in which Madeira benefits its neighborhood, the Co-curriculum is first. The achievements of girls in every class have been acknowledged by community organizations. In 1992 the J.C. Penney Golden Rule Youth Award went to a student volunteer in a crisis shelter for neglected and runaway teens. Every year Madeira girls have been recognized for ''outstanding community service'' by the local Rotary Club.

The other result relates to women in American society today. One can argue that women working as volunteers have changed America—from the colonial dames who boycotted British goods to antebellum abolitionists to suffragists to the veterans of Hull House who lobbied for pure food and drug laws, safer factories, shorter days and higher wages, kindergartens and child labor laws, to civil rights workers and peace marchers and environmental activists. But with a downturn in the economy and an increase in single female heads of house, women are staying in the paid work force. Who is taking their place in the volunteer sector? The answer may be young people—including Madeira girls on Wednesdays.

Because the Co-curriculum is a popular program which distinguishes Madeira from our competition, we tend to downplay the downside. The pluses are apparent; the minuses we accept. First among the "cons" is our 4-day school week. We are in class only Mondays, Tuesdays, Thursdays, and Fridays. This puts pressure on faculty and students alike to cover the same amount of material every other school does. Teaching is fast-paced and students are expected to keep up. We recite numbers of minutes in class as evidence that we are not shortchanging girls, and we count Co-curriculum days in our tally of total days in session per year. Based on Advanced Placement results and other measures, student performance is not handicapped by a so-called short week. (In fact, there are countervailing factors. Boarders especially like being off campus on Wednesdays and faculty have a designated work and committee meeting day.)

The second negative relates to evaluation. Completion of the Co-curriculum is a graduation requirement but performance is not graded. Pass, fail, and outstanding marks are given and supervisors write individual evaluations. If a student chooses to shortchange her Co-curriculum assignment, we follow up with all the usual academic consequences. Another concern is the safety factor. Three-quarters of the student body is off campus in someone else's care or on their own in an urban area full of temptations. Accountability is built into the program, including clear policies, procedures, and expectations and frequent contact between the school and intern supervisors. Inappropriate behavior while in Co-curriculum is one of eight major school rules, and could result in suspension or expulsion.

A third concern is that the Co-curriculum has made it more difficult for the school to require in-house community service—cleaning erasers, collecting lost belongings, recycling soda cans. Because girls "gave at Co-curriculum," they are less eager to accept another demand on an already full schedule. On the other hand, inspired by their Co-curriculum placements, students have independently organized a gleaning for food distribution programs at homeless shelters, a literacy corps of Saturday tutors, a special Olympics, and sandwich-making for soup kitchens.

The final cost of the Co-curriculum is its expense. Madeira employs two full-time, 12-month staff members to run the program. In addition to the selection and screening of placements, regular visits with supervisors and frequent interviews with students, this staff is responsible for the entire student body every Wednesday. Stipends are paid to some of the freshman program leaders, but the biggest expense is the buses hired to transport students.

None of this dissuades us, however. Madeira's Co-curriculum was the inspiration of Barbara Keyser, Headmistress from 1965–1978, who responded to President Kennedy's call to serve country and community. Lucy Madeira, the school's founder, would have applauded the idea. A Fabian socialist, an FDR democrat, and the public school-educated daughter of a boarding-house proprietor, Miss Madeira declared in 1925 that "the excuse for a private school in a democracy is that it shall be a laboratory, a place for demonstration of old experiments and the trying of new. It is a place of freedom."

Through the Co-curriculum at Madeira students serve their community, explore career options, learn and apply basic skills, reinforce work habits, make decisions, interact with adults, test values, and become competent, confident compassionate young women. They begin to see their whole lives as a co-curricular adventure.

4

Scheduling Options and Opportunities

by Steve Clem, Vice President for Educational Leadership
National Association of Independent Schools

Introduction: Perceptions and Realities

In Joseph Heller's novel of World War II, *Catch 22*, the protagonist, a bombardier named Yossarian, serves in a bomber group taking part in the fight to capture the city of Bologna. Because the anti-aircraft defenses were so strong and the bombing routes so predictable, each mission brought terrible losses in planes and men, but as long as the American ground troops had not taken the city, Yossarian's group would continue to fly missions over the city. A map of Italy had been put up so the pilots could follow the progress of the ground fighting by means of a ribbon that traced the advance of the troops. The ribbon soon became the focal point of the hopes and fears of the airmen, the men huddling around the map, willing the ribbon to move. While the ribbon was only a concrete representation of a distant reality, it became for the flyers the reality itself.

When night fell, they congregated in the darkness with their flashlights, continuing their macabre vigil at the bomb line in brooding entreaty as though hoping to move the ribbon up by the collective weight of their sullen prayers. "I really can't believe it," Clevinger exclaimed to Yossarian . . . "It's a complete reversion to primitive superstition. They're confusing cause and effect."

We can be equally mesmerized and duped by our school's schedule, seeing it as a reality unto itself, as more permanent and immutable than it really is. In fact, the schedule is an ephemeral construct that reflects many conscious and unconscious decisions, and that can be changed

37

rather easily, if we really want to change it. But first we have to be clear about what is cause and what is effect.

Does How We Make Changes Matter?

It is important to be very clear about one thing from the outset: how you go about creating your schedule is as important—I really wanted to say more important—than what you end up with: a highly traditional, unin-spired schedule that has been created in an inclusive and thoughtful way can be quite successful; a brilliant, ground-breaking schedule devised by one or two people in a closed room can be a total disaster before a single class has been held.

"Are You Free at . . . ?"

Scheduling a school is simply a very complicated attempt to arrange a set of meetings that a lot of people can attend. Think about how much harder it is to arrange a time to meet with six people than with two; the more people, the more variables. The more variables, the lower the success rate. If you do in fact find a time when all six people can meet, it's a safe bet that at least three of the people are not getting the meeting time they prefer (well, maybe it's two).

So think of your schedule as a whole series of meetings where you have to get fifteen to twenty people together at the same time in a space that will meet the needs of that particular meeting, with a chair who is com-petent to run the meeting. If you have ever had to run around frantically to schedule a meeting at school, you have some imperfect sense of what it feels like to build a schedule.

Uniqueness

Unlike public schools in which uniformity of program and resources across a district, or even a larger area, makes it relatively easy for one school's scheduling innovation to be adopted successfully by another school, independent schools are in many ways each a unique organism, more likely to reject than accept a transplant. Whatever the surface re-semblances, each school's schedule has its own unique genetic material, the templates that determine how the schedule will be structured.

It follows then that the drawback with outside consultants and store-bought schedules is that they can not possibly take into account all of the parameters that you are aware of. While you can certainly learn from what others do, you have to build your own schedule.

Leopards in the Temple

In a Kafka parable leopards break into the temple and drink all the ceremonial wine. When they do it a second year, they became part of the ritual. What leopards do you have in your school?

Time to Think

Nothing is in shorter supply in schools than time to think. (If we have time we'll double back and dwell on the irony of that statement.) For the moment, let's just say that the more time you can give your scheduling team to work on the schedule, the happier you will be with the results. There are always multiple possible solutions to scheduling problems. Given unlimited time and energy the schedulers will be able to identify many of them and choose the best. In the real world of schools, it is far more likely that the schedulers will feel that they will have to go with the first solution that occurs to them. Everyone then has to live with that decision, for better or for worse. With more time, less pressure, and others to bounce ideas off, the schedulers can do better.

Scheduling Savings Account

Keep a list of the ways you can help yourself and work towards realizing as many as you can. What can you do, for example, to gradually phase out your part-time teachers? Are there different ways to think about lunch? or physical education? or science labs? Could you make the school day twenty minutes longer? Rethink the major constraints. Are they truly immutable? Seek flexibility and put it in your "savings account" for when you may need it. Over the course of a year, three or four small deposits of flexibility may add up to a major scheduling nest egg. But you have to be looking for these occasions.

Are you making decisions elsewhere that will have an impact on your schedule? Yes! you are, but often you don't know it until it is too late. Try to foresee the possible scheduling consequences of certain actions. Be aware when you are making "withdrawals" from your account, and be sure that is how you want to spend your money.

Computers

Most schools report using the computer for some aspect of scheduling, and most of those report that they use the computer primarily for record keeping and the generation of lists. "I do the schedule by hand and then put it in the computer" is a common description. If you are not using the computer at all, push yourselves to get at least to the point where you can use the computer to do basics. By using either store-bought software or your own program try to get to the point where you can use the computer for generating a conflict matrix (an ongoing list of students or teachers who have schedule conflicts). Ironically the people who would most benefit—the schedulers—may be the most reluctant to take the computer plunge. If you've always done the schedule on the bulletin board in your office, or on the floor of your family room, it's hard to jump into doing it on the computer. It will take longer the first time you use the computer, and there will be problems, but you'll like the results, and you'll save a lot of time the second time around. The computer itself won't be shouting "Eureka!" but by making it far easier to try the "what ifs," it will increase the odds of those moments of insight. Check around. Find out what other people are using. Chances are that six weeks of research will yield some excellent leads. Buy the hardware and software you need and pay for training.

Scheduling Literacy

For some reason people in schools like to pretend that they could never possibly understand what scheduling is all about (We probably shouldn't rule out the possibility that they are afraid they'll be asked to do it), often acting quite silly about it. Schedulers sometimes contribute to this by acting as though there is some dark mystery involved. Scheduling can appear to be an arcane practice, a kind of impenetrable freemasonry with its own language, customs, and rituals. You need to demystify the process; not everybody can be a talented scheduler, but everybody can be brought to understand the basics.

The ultimate goal should be to raise the scheduling literacy of all staff, so that everyone can be part of the solutions or at least be intelligent consumers of the scheduling product. You also want to spread ownership and accountability so that people see it as "our" schedule—which, of course, it is. All faculty should, then, have Scheduling 101. Your scheduling advisory group needs the graduate work.

The Loneliness of the Scheduler

Many schedulers describe it as a lonely job. The scheduler's work is, at best, poorly grasped by his or her colleagues, if not actively resented, and even the scheduler's supervisor often does not really understand what is involved (So, how does one get good supervision?). People almost never notice the hard-won victories, but they will howl at the failures and never fully believe that anything was really unsolvable. Teachers who've ended up with a schedule they don't like will harbor the belief—often unfounded—that it didn't have to be that way. Because they don't really understand scheduling (raise their literacy!), their frustration is increased. The best way to fight this isolation is to create a scheduling advisory group.

Scheduling Group

You will be best served in your scheduling efforts if you create some kind of scheduling advisory group that meets on a regular basis throughout the year to think about scheduling issues. Thinking about the schedule should be a year-round process. If you only think about something important once a year, you severely restrict the number of helpful approaches you're likely to come up with. This group sets policy and priorities, explores options, and provides guidance for the actual schedulers. Get your most creative people in this group, your best problem-solvers. Do not assume that good schedulers can only be found in the math department, or that people who know how to use the computer are automatically good at generating scheduling solutions. The schedule is a place where you want to involve all the intelligences, seeking the synergy that will bring the best possible ideas to the fore. Support this team in every way possible. Have them set clear performance goals and ask them to be accountable.

Guess What They Want?
Ask Them What They Want?

This is a major, philosophical decision for schools (mostly middle and upper schools): build a schedule and then have students make choices (often called "arena scheduling"); or have students make requests and then build a schedule that honors as many of those as possible ("request-based scheduling").

Most of us are familiar with arena scheduling from our college experience where the college produced a catalogue with days and times for courses, and we built our schedules. We had the illusion of full choice in that we were picking our courses, but in reality many possibilities had been eliminated by those who built the schedule and made it impossible, for example, to take French Symbolist Poetry and Modern French Novel at the same time. Here's where *Catch 22* and the ribbon come in again: because the pre-established schedule seemed so formidable, so complicated, so totally immutable, so "printed," we accepted its reality far too easily and tended not to object or question the underlying assumptions. I took my poetry course and hoped that the next year I could do the novel course. Arena scheduling packs its own brand of fatalism and is a powerful ally of the status quo, tending to reinforce predictable patterns rather than honor anomalies. An illuminating exercise for those who use arena scheduling is to review the schedule from the perspective of all the things a given student cannot do, to tease out the hidden curriculum your schedule creates by default.

With request-based scheduling you encourage students to exercise at least some free will and sign up for the courses they really want from the menu of possibilities you present. And then you say you will do your best to make it all work. At this initial sign-up time there are far fewer conflicts; no student has to choose between computer science and studio art, at least not yet. Inevitably, of course, there are conflicts, and some students end up with their second or third choices.

I believe that with request-based scheduling more kids get what they want. The catch—and there is always a catch—is that with request-based scheduling you know your failure rate, and the disappointments are sharper because you have created greater expectations. With arena scheduling you don't know the failure rate, because you never gave the students a chance to say what they wanted. You simply told them what they could have. If you use request-based scheduling, and most schools do, at least to some extent you must explain and sell the approach.

Choices

Giving kids and parents choices is good, but it's more complicated than no choices. It is also far less predictable. If you only offer Spanish in the middle school and everybody has to take it, then you know how many sections and how many teachers you need. If you offer Spanish and French and kids coming into the middle school can sign up for either, you have created at least the potential for serious scheduling and personnel problems. If you then build in the possibility of switching languages and also agree to creating an honors section for eighth grade Spanish, you will have painted yourself into a very tough corner; your language courses may end up driving the whole schedule.

Now, this may not be a bad thing. The key is that these be conscious choices and that your constituents understand the possible implications. Think these decisions through carefully before you go ahead and do it, remembering how hard it can be to change later: "Well, they have to be in an honors course. Do you want to hold them back?"

It is also possible to offer too much choice. Combining, say, a commitment to giving students exactly what they want with a dizzying array of semester electives in tenth and eleventh grade English is a formula for craziness, unless you are willing to have these electives determine everything else (and then you may have a host of other disasters on your hands). Think of proliferating electives as further withdrawals from your scheduling savings account.

Remember that we have the honorable, but often misguided, tendency to keep adding more and more things to our program because it seemed like a good idea. No school can possibly accommodate all the good ideas people can come up with, and teach everything that students might need to know.

Scheduling Constituencies

We tend to see faculty as the main consumers of the schedule, probably because we hear the most from them, and they squeal the loudest when something doesn't work. This may be a little skewed. Imagine Ford deciding that they should pay more attention to their dealers than their customers. Aim to create a better level of scheduling literacy among students and, to a lesser degree, parents. Articulate your scheduling philosophy clearly to your constituents; educate parents and students. Be sure they understand the trade-offs. If you don't have a scheduling philosophy, get one. Every school ought to be able to articulate how its schedule supports and furthers its mission.

The Real Conflicts Come Before
You Schedule Anything

Stark economic realities will often clash with other scheduling priorities: the most basic example is the school that has to cover two sections of math with a part-time teacher who can/will only work mornings. This reduces sharply the possibilities of creating, for example, a rotating schedule that allows for real variety in the times that classes meet. The difference between the full-time and part-time hire might be $15,000. So for the cost of one or two tuitions the school has to make a decision that potentially disadvantages all of its students. Of course, if you can't come up with the $15,000, this can't be helped. But are you sure you can't? Are you sure you have thought of all the other possible ways to cover those two sections?

If It's Monday, It Must Be Monday

Independent schools are in near total thrall to the five-day cycle. The vast majority of schools have chosen to stick with a five-day cycle despite the very real advantages that come with a longer cycle. The reason this gets voted down in most places is that the adults in the school are afraid it will be too confusing, that they won't be able to learn the new system ("I'll never know what day it is!"). Bear in mind that we're talking about schools here! Imagine our response if the ninth grade decided that they weren't going to read *Romeo and Juliet* because it was too hard to learn. This is not to say that a six-day cycle is for everyone, but don't reject it just because some people are afraid they can't learn it.

How Long Is a Period?

Why is a forty-two minute class perfectly acceptable while a thirty-nine minute class is not? What is the magic of the forty minute boundary? We have forty-two minute classes not because we really believe that that is how students will learn best, but rather because we have too many things to fit into the day; so we cut up the day into little pieces. And we make ourselves feel good about this by holding to the forty minute limit tenaciously. This is like what happens when we're doing something we know we shouldn't do (fill in your own example), but we try to compensate by doing it a little bit less or by making up byzantine rules to govern the behavior ("I'm going to eat the last three brownies, but I'll close my eyes").

Do we really believe that students learn best in forty minute periods punctuated by frantic running around? If you believe that, then you've probably got the right schedule. But if you don't. . . .

Schools need to find ways of providing longer chunks of time for better teaching and learning. The typical student only gets sustained time for learning in athletics, the arts, or other co-curricular activities; the debater, the field hockey player, the actor, or the dancer may have as long as three hours per day to learn and practice skills. The typical English student gets forty-five minutes, plus homework time. And most work in athletics and the arts is profoundly social and collaborative, unlike most academic work. Why can't we/won't we transfer what we know in athletics and the arts to academics?

Deal with This if You Want to Get Anywhere (But Be Ready to Feel Some Pain)

One significant way to gain scheduling flexibility and give students a little breathing space is to have classes not meet every day. But just to mention the idea in some circles is rankest heresy. There is a common, unshakable, view that in subject X (fill in the subject you teach) the students must have class every day to learn. This is not, of course, an irrational belief. Nor is it necessarily true. Is time really the crucial factor in good learning? Accepting for the moment that less time is, in fact, a handicap, is it not possible that one could compensate for less time with better curriculum, better teaching, and more thoughtful out-of-class work?

This gets to the schedule as your salary scale for time. No one ever is willing to take a cut in salary. We also get ourselves into a big "fairness" thing. And "fair" usually ends up meaning equal time for everything, whether that makes good pedagogical sense or not. Sometimes "fair" just means easier or less painful.

Let's Make the School Year Longer

A wonderful idea if done for the right reasons and in the right way. My guess is that if most schools added ten days to their year, most would use those ten days to do more of the SOT (same old thing), instead of, for example, using the extra time to relax the frantic pace of the year and consider things in greater depth. The classic response of teachers to news that classes will be longer next year, is "Great, now we can cover more." Howard Gardner says that we need to do fewer things in school, not more:

> The greatest enemy of understanding is coverage. As long as you are determined to cover everything, you actually ensure that most kids are not going to understand . . . Now this is the most revolutionary idea is American education—because most people can't abide the notion that we might leave out one decade of American history or one formula or one biological system. But that's crazy, because we now know that kids don't understand those things anyway. They forget them as soon as the test is over. (*Educational Leadership*, April, 1993)

Find a Way to Do This

Getting your schedule done before the end of the present school year is enormously helpful; people have time to solve problems and adjust to what's coming. Both students and teachers really like knowing their schedules before the start of summer vacation.

Making Compromises

Scheduling is a long series of compromises. It is interesting to note that the connotations, the affect of the word *compromise,* have seemed to vary over time, from the negative (compromise = surrender) to the positive (compromise = getting to yes). In a sense, once the first block of the schedule is put in place, the first "singleton" scheduled, everything else is a compromise.

Making Decesions

When you have to make tough choices (Does middle school language arts get that two-period block, or does middle school math meet every day?), you have to be clear about how you will make the decision.

Ideally, you will be making most of these decisions based on your beliefs and assumptions about the nature of the learning process for children. This seems obvious, but you can't do this if you have not, as an institution, clarified your beliefs about the nature of the learning process and the conditions under which it is most likely to occur. People's eyes start to glaze over at this point, but you have to have some benchmark, or you'll be the playthings of contingency and office politics, and things will fall apart.

SHORT FORM: BASIC ADVICE

- Program must drive schedule; if you believe that and act on it, you can make things happen. Otherwise you will be driven by the weight of the schedule.
- Avoid the pathetic fallacy when talking about the schedule ("The schedule won't allow it!"). The schedule is not a sentient creature. To dissociate it from the people and the decisions that created it is already to have given up some power over it.
- Sometimes you can change the rules, and sometimes far more easily than you think.
- If you don't have a scheduling philosophy, get one.
- Think of the scheduling process as an extraordinary opportunity and not just a tedious chore. It is, after all, the structure of your work and learning for the next year.
- Make sure you know your constraints, and make sure they are real.
- Virtually any decision about program, personnel, or facilities will have a scheduling price tag. Be sure you know what it is in advance and that your constituents understand what you are getting for that price.
- With no benchmarks to help you arbitrate conflicts, the loudest, most obnoxious, most persistent, or most respected people tend to dominate the scheduling process; and the respected person may be just as wrong as the obnoxious person. Be clear about your educational goals and priorities.
- Multiple-division schools must work hard to prevent one division's needs or preferences from regularly taking precedence (usually it's the upper school). Should, for example, AP Biology labs dictate— through labyrinthine trails of cause and effect—when fifth graders have lunch?
- Occam's Razor may be pleasing on some philosophical level, but often in scheduling the simplest solution is not the best.

- Understand that the real action is in the decisions and priorities that inform the schedule, not the schedule itself. Push yourselves hard to think broadly and clearly about what you really want your curriculum to be before you even start to think about your schedule. Know what you want.
- Better schedules mean better teaching and learning.

5

Marketing Schools: Using Your Current Audience To Build the Next One

by Kathleen O'Neill Jamieson, Director of Admission
Princeton Day School

There are plenty of workshops out there on marketing schools. Participants generally nod their heads a lot and recognize plenty of good ideas and familiar issues. What never seems to emerge is the organizing principle to set a plan in motion. To mobilize your school's constituencies as marketing agents, consider creating equal but distinct plans for three groups of people:

1. Loyal Supporters—Internal representatives

- administrators and faculty
- current parents
- current students
- trustees.

2. Hot Prospects—The current candidate pool

- leads, new inquiries, applicants, accepted, rejected, waiting list, enrolled, refused.

3. Community Leaders—External representatives

- local alumni
- past parents

- local educators
- corporate employees
- religious leaders
- extracurricular program directors
- other non-profit directors.

Before any effective planning takes place, you'll have to have your admission office calendar under control. Review month-to-month admission office activity or begin charting it. Busy admission officers must be expert time managers in order to market effectively the institution while providing professional level counseling for families. Also, gather all relevant research: attrition figures, demographic information, and five-year applicant pool.

Avoid the temptation to neglect your internal and external representatives in favor of the current candidate pool. If necessary, place the three action plans on the wall. Be sure staff meetings and administrative meetings include answers to the following questions:

1. Do my internal people know what to do this month?
2. Are we paying the right kind of attention to our candidates? Who needs to do what when?
3. Do our external representatives have a message to deliver? How are they getting it, and are they delivering it?

Internal Action

Faculty members are at once the most natural marketers of schools and the least effective. While they have first-hand knowledge of the opportunities available for students, they operate with very limited information about policies and procedures regarding admissions. Consequently, they avoid playing the recruitment role they are so capable of playing.

Ask any admission officer about the most effective referral system and chances are they'll tell you that word-of-mouth parental referral is the most valuable. Not only are parents the most frequent source of inquiries, but the conversion from inquiry to enrolled student is highest when a current parent sends a student in the school's direction. Current students, faculty, administrators, and trustees are additional underutilized fans.

To maximize the potential benefit of the internal people as ''marketers,'' the school must provide representatives with three things:

1. information
2. personal satisfaction with the institution
3. the opportunity to serve.

Information

Try the following set of questions on a random sample of your faculty:

- What is the annual tuition cost?
- What kind of financial aid program do you have?
- What is the admission process?
- Why do parents choose your school?

The wide range of responses and the degree of uncertainty expressed at most schools is indicative of a marketing plan gone awry—leaving insiders out of the loop.

A similar set of questions could be asked of parents, students, or trustees. The point is that the school needs to develop and control the appropriate message.

Be sure to use school publications and events to update faculty, parents, and trustees. Plan feature articles and oral presentations to hit on key themes on a regular basis.

Personal Satisfaction/Parents and Faculty

Parents and faculty members will help you market your school as long as they are personally satisfied. If their experience of the institution is positive, they will be natural marketers, responding openly and enthusiastically when given the opportunity to talk about your school. On the other hand, there is no more damaging message than the criticism of responsible parents and faculty members who are dissatisfied, disenfranchised or apathetic.

- How do you know if your faculty members are satisfied?
- How do you know if your parents are satisfied?

A comprehensive marketing plan will include means to evaluate the satisfaction of various constituencies. Focus groups, surveys, town meetings, and personal conferences are possible research tools generally available to schools. Use them. As you reach out to your parents and faculty members, you will see them reaching back.

To engage the support of parents and faculty, the school has several jobs to do. First, those who are invited to join the parent or faculty constituency must be fully informed of the philosophy and expectations of the school. Second, the school should have a schedule of events and communications designed specifically to affirm parents' and teachers' decision to support the school. Third, the school's leaders must seek the counsel of these important constituencies in a systematic way. In addition, these leaders should pursue a reputation for keeping those closest to the school well-informed of current issues and future plans.

Opportunity to Serve

Be sure to present clear opportunities to serve the school. Offer individuals the chance to specify in what way they would like to offer their time or expertise. For example, talk to faculty members about options and then give them a sign-up sheet with choices such as interviewing candidates, planning divisional events, hosting events, posting announcements of events, visiting feeder schools, making follow-up phone calls to candidates, traveling to school fairs, etc.

Parent volunteers may have similar options. In addition, you might want to recruit neighborhood hostesses, elicit the help of corporate contacts, or garner *pro bono* services related to marketing and communications. Whatever you do, don't ignore offers to help. If you arouse interest from volunteers, you better be prepared to use them and manage them well. That means you must identify a specific role for the volunteer, communicate often enough to assess his or her level of service and commitment, and then acknowledge volunteer effort both privately and publicly.

Your goal is to have a majority contribute some energy, no matter how little, to the marketing effort. The act of participating will increase awareness and sensitivity to their power as school representatives; loyalty to the institution will also grow.

Candidate Pool

These are the hot prospects who have landed in your admission office, thanks to the successful effort of a well-informed and highly motivated group of internal and external school representatives! Consider the following needs:

- to educate families about independent education
- to help parents and students develop points of comparison between your school and others

- to evaluate the students in relation to curriculum
- to motivate families to complete the admission process
- to meet enrollment targets.

The ideal admission process reflects the philosophy of the school. Try designing your process with a couple of imagined quotations in mind. What do you want families to tell their friends and neighbors about their experience with your school?

"I learned more about my child from the interviewer than I've learned from teachers in five years."

"Student tour guides were able to show me just how special the school is. You couldn't miss the school's philosophy in action."

"My child wasn't accepted, but the admission office gave us very specific information that we've been searching for."

This approach helps to match the admission process to the real values of the school and avoids the risk of an admission process that just adds layers: more letters, more invitations, more follow-up by well-wishers. The admission process itself becomes a marketing tool when guided by the following principles:

- Admission officers represent the quality of faculty.
- Recruitment materials reflect the values of the school and communicate expertise in areas such as child development, curriculum development, learning disabilities, and teacher training.
- Orientation programs are designed to introduce students and parents to the culture of the school and encourage newcomers to bring their good ideas with them.
- Feedback is expected. New families are invited to discuss their earliest experiences with the school in focus groups, phone interviews and town meetings.

For every action in the admission office there is an appropriate reaction. A good exercise for the admission staff is to make decisions about what should happen to whom when.

Here are some examples:

New Inquiry   Receives admission materials within 48 hours

Applicant   Receives a phone call from a division head or a letter from the headmaster.

Referrer	Receives a phone call and personal note from the admission director thanking the person for the referral and promising an update.
30-Day-Old Inquiry	Receives a second mailing which calls for action: an invitation, the return of a response card.
Accepted Student Who Refuses Offer	Receives a call from admission director who investigates reasons for decision and invites family to future school events.
Alumni Candidate	In addition to admission materials parents receive a call from the head of the alumni council.
Rejected	Parents receive a call in advance. Student receives rejection letter with specific reasons for reject.
Non-local Candidate	Receives a video tape along with catalog.
Unresponsive Inquiry	Receives a letter and reply card with a request for information regarding decision not to apply.

Each school will have a unique set of cases and should tailor responses to fit the character of the school. Even the smallest staff with limited resources can establish a consistent pattern of responses to families moving through the admission office. Remember to keep it clear and simple. You don't want to distract your audience with public relations highjinks.

Never forget that you are pitching to parents looking for a school for their children. Marketing plans begin with the educational standards of the school and the administration's commitment to meet those standards.

Once the admission office has enrolled students, the work to retain them begins. In essence, the baton is then handed from the admission officer to the division head. While the admission officer orchestrates meetings on attrition in relation to enrollment targets, all administrators should recognize their role in lowering attrition:

- Job descriptions for all administrators should include marketing responsibility.
- A watch list should be reviewed regularly to determine which students may transfer.

- Families relocating should receive assistance in finding new schools.
- Students being counseled to other schools should have advance notice in writing and support from the admission office in finding a new school.

Too many schools worry about "managing attrition," rather than lowering attrition. School with healthy attrition rates share the following tenets:

- Practice what you preach in your catalog.
- Be sure the division heads are as alert to consumer needs as the admission officers.
- Establish standards for all communications—from teacher handouts to headmaster's letters.
- Do unto others . . . return the phone call today!
- Pay attention to each family's connection to the school.

External Representatives

Assume that the community is asking questions about your school. What does the school care about? What does the school give? What does it take? What does it need? What does it want? Whom does it serve?

Community leaders are answering these questions, whether you like it or not. What can you do to increase your confidence that community leaders are sending the right messages?

Here's the third leg of your marketing triangle. Devise a plan to canvass the community with good and accurate news about your institution and private education in general:

- Assign administrators responsibility in the community (Chamber of Commerce, Jaycees, various boards, feeder schools, arts organizations).
- Develop programs which include students from the community (summer camp, after-school care).
- Invite business people to campus (speakers' bureau, luncheon with headmaster, realtor's reception).
- Send a catalog to parents and local alumni with reply cards for referrals.
- Remember LOCAL community service opportunities for students.
- Invest in direct mail lists and target your audience.

- Make advertising decisions; don't just advertise.
- Ask local experts for advice—build relationships.
- Attend educational and business functions.
- Make it easy to visit; consider working couples.

Your weekly goals should always include progress with external relations. Keep a running list of valuable contacts and rotate calls and meetings throughout the year.

Your network will develop quickly and the calls will begin to go both ways.

Feeder Schools

Your relationships with other schools are perhaps the most valuable in the community. Don't take them for granted. School counselors aren't going to remember how you treated the candidate; they're going to remember how you treated them:

- Did you acknowledge information sent?
- Did you inform sending school of admission decision?
- Did you maintain confidentiality of a recommendation?
- Have counselors been invited to campus?

Admission officers and faculty members should devote significant time to school visits in the fall. Counselors can provide important information to help you anticipate the transition kids are making from a previous school. In addition, your observations will make you more effective in parent conferences throughout the year.

Analyze the success of students entering from various schools. Start by asking your teachers to look at students by the sending school, and ask if they can make any generalizations about their preparation, motivation, and aptitude.

Good relationships with feeder schools lead to:

- dependable recommendations
- appropriate referrals
- pre-admission support, such as tutorials
- excellent word-of-mouth
- confidence of families applying.

Similar goals can be set for other organizations within the community. Ballet schools, karate clubs, libraries, learning centers, and sport leagues all offer recruitment opportunities. Start small and engage one faculty member after another, one trustee after another, and one alumnus after another to assume responsibility for attracting the most suitable student body possible.

Each community offers possibilities for advancement. By analyzing and responding to the unmet needs of families within your community, your school can build a reputation as an educational leader.

6

Parent Relations

by Arlene F. Hogan, Head of School &
Nancy S. Kami, Director of Development
The Hamlin School

The New Parent Partners

"For me, the ideal private school would consist entirely of independently wealthy orphans," so lamented one school head who was in his own words, "fed up dealing with demanding, obnoxious parents."

Undoubtedly, the care and treatment of independent school parents in the 90s is a major challenge for all schools. Whether these parents become our adversaries or our allies has much to do with how we educate, engage, and acknowledge this important constituency. A different breed entirely from parents of twenty years ago, most experience their first independent school through their child. Seeking an alternative from what they perceive to be unsafe and ineffective public schools, they arrive with great expectations at the doorsteps of schools like ours. Paradoxically, independent schools are more familiar, and perhaps more comfortable, with the "traditional" private school family in which one or both parents, or even grandparents, are products of this system. No need to explain how the game is played to these folks. They may grumble at times, but without a doubt you'll receive their annual giving check, their support for the capital campaign, and a tacit acknowledgement that your school knows what it's doing in educating their children. In addition, they understand the need to volunteer.

How can you ensure that the new constituency of parents, those encountering private school for the first time, becomes your school's strongest proponent, rather than your biggest headache? Experience at our own school as well as observation of other well-run independent schools confirms the need for ongoing parent education.

Imagine starting school next week in a foreign country. You would have little or no idea of the customs, the habits, the rules. If no one sat down with you to *explain* the culture, your discomfort would only increase. It would become increasingly difficult for you to place your trust in or feel a part of an institution you didn't "understand."

This is not so different from what it is like for the new parent entering independent schools. What are the rules here? What are the stated and the implied expectations of parents? What constitutes parent involvement? At what point does involvement become interference? In order to make everyone feel comfortable and to encourage appropriate involvement, all this needs to be explained clearly and often to your parent group.

The Admission Process

Begin educating parents at the beginning. It is vital to have an effective admissions office that brings in the kinds of families who are "good" for your school. Admissions officers need to look for parents who convey cooperation, trust in the school, and a sense of responsibility to the school whether it be in supporting its policies or its Annual Fund. You're admitting the family, not just the student. Admissions must look beyond the immediate enrollment of the student to the future. Can we live with this family for the next . . . years? Will they be "happy," and will we?

The admission process is the ideal time to educate parents. It is only fair to let parents know of the philosophical and financial support that the school expects from them. Discuss the culture of your school, its mission, the role parents play, and the general policies parents and students are expected to honor.

Welcoming New Families

Asking board members to call new parents immediately upon their child's acceptance by your school conveys a warm and friendly welcome. A reception for new parents in all grades hosted by current parents helps to introduce them to the school community. Creating a "buddy system" by pairing current families as hosts for new families helps to ease new families into the school community. If the partners in the buddy system are determined the summer prior to the new student's entrance, the school increases the potential for interaction between the new families and their soon-to-be classmates and class parents. This strategy also lessens any anxiety the student and his or her parents may experience prior to the start of school.

New Parent Orientation

The orientation of parents new to your school can make or break future relationships. Provide a formal orientation for new parents at all grade levels, led by members of the administration, including the head, division director, director of development, parent association head and appropriate faculty members. Remember, questions and concerns can range from the most basic, "What should Sally bring for lunch?" to the complex, "Can you ensure that my kindergartner will get into Harvard?" Encouraging all types of questions helps to reassure parents and prevent misunderstandings and misdirected energy.

In addition to setting a positive tone, the orientation should also set limits. For example, instructing parents regarding visits to the student's class: e.g., some schools have an open-door/drop-in type arrangement, others require scheduled visits. Explain how the lines of communication at the school work so that parents may have their questions, suggestions, or concerns addressed. Be sure that every faculty member is clear on the system and cooperates with it. If you tell parents that their first call should be to their child's homeroom teacher, you must be sure that the teacher returns the calls he or she receives in a timely manner. Responding to concerns immediately puts out potential fires before they flame.

The orientation is also a good time to review the school's policy on issues such as discipline, drugs and alcohol. In addition, details such as proper attire, uniform requirements, carpool rules, etc., should be reviewed. Providing a comprehensive overview of the school community reassures parents and helps them to feel more comfortable in the new situation. Also explain the different fund-raising activities which parents will encounter throughout the year, so they know what to expect and what is expected of them.

On-Going Communication

Orientation for new parents is only the first step in their education. Since people tend to hear what they want to hear, repetition is the key to getting your message across. Consider every school year to be a new beginning and assume no one remembers anything from the year before. Remind parents frequently of the school's expectations and policies as they were articulated at the opening parent orientation. If you make the effort consistently, the information you want to convey will sink in. Communicate often in memos, letters, newsletters and meetings.

Encourage parents to communicate with you. An "open-door" policy for the head and other administrators gives parents the opportunity to address issues directly with the appropriate person. Too often questions or misunderstandings quickly become major issues and hot rumors for parents to fuel chatting at the local grocery store. How frustrating it is to hear thirdhand that a bunch of parents are upset by the math program in the 3rd grade! It must be stressed that such concerns need to be brought directly to the school so they can be dealt with forthwith, not spread anonymously and sometimes viciously in the community where they cannot be addressed.

The Not-So-New Parents' Orientation

Annual grade-level meetings in September for all parents, similar to the new parent orientation, help to reassure and reeducate all parents and to provide a forum for new issues which arise as the student progresses to the next grade level. Remember to review the same issues which are addressed at the New Parent Orientation, and explain any changes in personnel, curriculum and policies so that everyone hears the same story and has the opportunity to have questions addressed by the school.

When issues arise throughout the year which concern an entire class or group of parents, make sure the information is communicated clearly, directly and in a timely manner to the parents. Holding meetings for all those involved or affected to discuss these concerns helps to ensure that the situation is understood. There is then a great likelihood parents will be supportive of the school's actions.

Publicizing Opportunities to Volunteer

What better way to be involved in your child's education than by volunteering at his or her school. There have been many studies conducted which indicate that students whose parents are active at their school become greater achievers and experience greater self-esteem. Offering plenty of opportunities for volunteering makes it easy for parents who want to be involved to participate in a structured and positive way that supports the school's goals. This avoids having them create their own, often destructive form of involvement. Send out volunteer sign-up sheets clearly explaining the various volunteer opportunities for parents, the estimated time commitment, and the way in which the activity supports the school. Call parents with particular skills to encourage their involvement. Have parents who are already volunteering call new parents to invite them to participate.

Parent Handbook

The bible for your school, the Parent Handbook, should spell out for everyone all the rules, expectations and procedures. Parents should be requested to sign an acknowledgement that they have read the handbook. There are countless times during the year when there is reason to refer parents to their handbook as a reminder for proper procedures. Make the handbook attractive, informative and readable. Many schools include their student rosters.

Directing Parents' Efforts

Undirected parent efforts often—usually—end up proceeding in the *wrong* direction. Areas where parents are useful to the school can be clearly outlined, and parent energy can be directed in specific ways creating a welcoming school environment where both the parent volunteers and the school benefit. Keep in mind that the new independent school parent doesn't necessarily fit the traditional family model. Therefore, while the independent school pool of volunteer parents continues to be dominated largely by women who are at home for a temporary period while they are raising young children, two-career couples, single parent households, and all variations of the non-traditional family need to be taken into account as you identify volunteer opportunities.

If your parent association is perceived as a "select" group that welcomes only a segment of your school's parent population, e.g. mothers who are homemakers, then you run the risk of alienating a significant pool of talent and energy. Two career couples, single parents, and fathers all can and should play a key role in the volunteer life of your school. It is up to the school's administration to oversee the leadership of the parents association, ensuring sensitivity to all forms of diversity in the parent body.

Remember, too, that volunteer participation creates a positive involvement with the school and is a very effective form of cultivation. When parents perceive themselves as valued contributors to the school as volunteers, it is much more likely that they will be contributors to the school's financial life as well, supporting the annual fund and other important fundraising activities. In giving their time, talent, and financial resources they become community members in a lasting and meaningful way.

Some schools find it helpful to establish a mandatory number of required hours of voluntary service per family. Establishing a realistic figure that all families can meet enables everyone to feel that they are making a valuable contribution to the school community and the education of their children.

Volunteer Opportunities to Consider

1. *Leadership*: A volunteer in a leadership position can make or break the organization. Good leaders make a world of difference and are not easy to find; ineffective or disruptive leaders can destroy the good will and support of your community. Choose carefully and thoughtfully—an unknown quantity is not necessarily better than a vacancy.

    Make sure there is a strong nominating committee that understands the importance of its role and the nuances involved, and works very closely with the Director of Development and Head in nominating parents for leadership roles. Leaders must be able to represent the school in a positive way, effectively lead peer parents and understand their responsibilities to the school. A great leader will not only be successful in fund-raising, but equally important, in friend-raising from your parents. A happy parent association is a valuable ambassador of good will to your broader community and admissions pool.

2. *Fund-Raising and School Events*: Offer volunteer opportunities which range from leadership participation to committing a few hours for stuffing envelopes. No job is insignificant. Often the next

leader of your Parents Association will be clearly identifiable after he or she has worked on a major fundraising event. Make it easy— provide the office support and background work that they need to do their jobs.

Appeal to the different needs and circumstances of your volunteers. Offer opportunities to socialize for those who have the time and enjoy teamwork and meeting people. This can include meetings set at convenient times, perhaps a breakfast, dessert or brainstorming get-together (feed them well!) that enables both spouses, working parents, and those with childcare responsibilities to participate. Volunteers who do not have the time for meetings or extra events will appreciate opportunities to be involved by working from their homes or offices, or taking on jobs that require a minimum commitment of hours, such as stuffing invitations, participating in a phonathon, or working a few hours at an event.

Utilize the talents of your parents by involving them in activities which benefit from their special skills and knowledge. For example, invite creative and artistic parents to contribute by designing programs and invitations for fund-raising events, providing homemade food for parties, creating centerpieces to sell, or sharing their talents with students. Encourage working parents to mentor students or speak to them about their careers. They can also be very helpful in soliciting underwriting or donations from corporate contacts and businesses.

The school should clearly define the purpose of fund-raising efforts prior to the events to eliminate confusion and misdirected use of funds raised. This also helps to promote events and gives volunteers a sense of ownership and responsibility. In addition, having the president of the Parent Association as an ex-officio member of the Board helps to convey the important role the Parent Association plays in supporting the school's mission and provides the president with an understanding of how the school operates.

3. *Annual Fund*: Many parents enjoy the opportunity to directly raise funds for the school and to work with fellow class parents toward a common goal. As class representatives for the Annual Fund, volunteers use their talent and time to raise critically needed funds for the school. The Annual Fund should be well-organized so that it is easy for volunteers to fulfill their responsibilities and ensure that they feel supported, productive and proud of their involvement. An added benefit to involving parents as Annual Fund volunteers is the

leadership gifts that often come from those who volunteer and feel committed to the program. Good Annual Fund solicitors can be tapped later as Capital Campaign volunteers or potential Board members. The Annual Fund provides volunteers with an involvement in the community without requiring the numerous meetings that many working parents may find cumbersome about other volunteer opportunities.

Educating Parents

As schools concentrate on developing self-esteem in students, volunteer opportunities, particularly in a leadership capacity, afford parents a unique opportunity to enhance their self-esteem as they face new challenges. Research indicates that perhaps at no other time in a woman's life is she less self-assured than when she chooses to stay home and raise a young family full-time. Despite the satisfaction that results from nurturing her family, a woman who left a career where she enjoyed a certain amount of power and autonomy as well as the day-to-day positive interaction with other adults may begin to doubt her own ability in the "outside world" when she is housebound for a period of time.

Volunteer opportunities providing challenge, recognition, and a chance to develop new skills often strike a perfect balance for this group. Flexible hours and the spectra of accomplishing important tasks for the school can have great appeal.

We are all too familiar with the mother who enjoyed an intense, successful career only to turn her intensity to the raising of her child with the same ardor. Over-involvement by parents in their children's lives can often prove as destructive as under-involvement. Again, worthwhile volunteer programs have the means to siphon off this energy in a positive fashion.

Modesty and lack of confidence often prevent parents from making volunteer commitments, especially those in leadership capacity. Encourage parents who you feel can do the job well. It may take some doing, as we have found, but almost always benefits the parent and the school in the end. Some of our most effective and outstanding volunteers have been the ones who said for years that they would never take on a leadership position because they were afraid of the pressures and time commitments involved. We have watched these parents blossom during their tenure in leadership positions, brimming with self-confidence and devoted commitment to the school after completing a successful job.

Offer "continuing education programs" for parents to provide an opportunity for them to learn how to be more effective parents. Parenting classes, seminars conducted by outside experts, speaker series featuring faculty members discussing new developments in their fields, are often of great interest to parents. Parent newsletters also keep everyone abreast of issues that are not just school-related, like where to find good summer camp programs. Parent education programs benefit the school by creating more effective parents and by providing positive public relations.

Appreciating Parents

In dealing with parent volunteers, the golden rule is never miss an opportunity to say "thank you." By acknowledging, recognizing and thanking them, you convey the school's appreciation for the important contributions they make to the school. Say it publicly and often, using all means at your disposal to do so: personal notes, special assemblies, newsletters, magazines, and other publications.

Involve the whole school in recognizing your volunteers, including Board members, faculty/staff, and students. A meaningful "thank you" and expression of appreciation encourages volunteers to continue their support. Public recognition of volunteers also engenders appreciation from fellow parents, and makes volunteering at the school inviting.

Handled with care, the new parent partners will become your school's most valued friends so that you can concentrate on running your school, and not wishing you ran an orphanage!

7

All Their Days

by Richard Barnhardt
Assistant Headmaster for External Affairs
Woodberry Forest School

In the corridor near my office is a large photo of the great throng of people who attended our school's centennial celebration. Alumni who encounter this photo always stop to find themselves or others whom they know. Recognitions bring smiles and recollections and illustrate what I think is a fundamental truth in alumni relations: Whenever alumni return to our schools, they want to find themselves.

It is not just nostalgia, although that certainly is at work and is heightened by the flow of young and unknown faces all around them. They are looking to find themselves in a larger context, that of a community in which they have not only a valued place in the school's past but also a meaningful role in the school's present and future. The principal goal of a school's alumni relations program is to foster a sense of community based on both shared experiences and shared interests.

Alumni are naturally bound together by their school experiences, which though intense and highly personal, they share in kind if not also in common with all of the school's alumni. One major thrust of our alumni relations program is to reveal how much of the school experience remains the same from one era to another. To do this we have made a significant investment in our school archives where we preserve and display school documents, photos, and memorabilia and from which we constantly draw material for publications and for display around the school campus. Not only does the archive material recognize and celebrate the past, thereby enabling alumni to quite literally find themselves at the school, it also expands the students' perspective of time and the character of their era. It makes them aware that they too are writing a chapter in a continuing story.

With its focus on the past, the archives encompass only half of the alumni experience. The other half is the present. In its relations with alumni a school should aim to take the same active interest in them as it did when they were students. This is a herculean task, but it is the very essence of good alumni relations. It is also closely related to a most practical need to maintain good, accurate, and up-to-date information on the alumni. The need for and utility of such information are so apparent ˙ that it is almost not worth mentioning, but mention it I must. Every school, regardless of its age or size, must have absolute control of its alumni records into which flows a constant stream of new information and from which emanate all of our communications with alumni. The alumni community is a large network at the center of which is the school's alumni office, the hub of a communications system whereby alumni maintain contact with each other and with the school.

Our alumni office begins collecting information when a student enrolls. His parents complete a detailed questionnaire that includes information about their employment, their other children, and their alumni connections. We also ask for the grandparents' names and addresses and for the names of hometown daily and weekly newspapers, useful to us when we send out press releases about the student's accomplishments. We update this information every year by sending a printout to the parents and asking them to notify us if there have been any changes. When a student graduates or otherwise leaves school, information from his academic file— application and official correspondence—is added to the files we maintain on each alumnus, files that over time can become thick with news clippings, photos, and copies of significant correspondence between the alumnus and school personnel. These files are the ultimate point of reference for us in working with our alumni and are an invaluable resource for understanding an almnus' relationship with the school, for producing a profile of or introduction for him, and for communicating with his family and writing his obituary for publication in our alumni magazine. The value of this information for donor research and for preparation of gift proposals is obvious.

Only essential information of current value, however, is entered into our computer data base. It must be entered accurately and kept as current as possible. Nothing is more irritating to an alumnus than to see his name misspelled, to be omitted from a list of donors, or to have things mailed to him at an address that he had informed us had changed. With only 365 students our school is a comparatively small one; our alumni expect us to know them. They are nonplussed by the old bureaucratic excuse that the computer has made an error. Inevitably, however, there are mistakes on our part as well as theirs. The most common misunderstanding we encounter stems from confusion about the beginning and end of our annual giving year, which parallels the school year rather than the calendar tax year. Complaints must be addressed immediately and forthrightly. A quick telephone call from someone the alumnus knows is usually the best approach.

Our database is useful to the alumni themselves and provides us with a highly valuable tool in our alumni relations program. Every five years we publish at school expense a complete alumni directory which we send free of charge to every alumnus of record. In addition to class and geographical listings, the main alphabetical listing provides the alumnus' full name, his address, and his home and office telephone numbers. Although everyone in our office becomes involved in proofing the copy, only two people are actually needed to produce the directory: the person who controls our alumni database and the person who uses our desktop publishing software to produce camera-ready copy for the printer. We prefer to produce our directory in-house because it reduces both the expense, which we spread over five years, and the opportunity for errors. Directories produced by external agents are less accurate and complete, take longer to produce, and are more expensive; moreover, they are usually available only to those alumni willing to pay for them.

In our directory we include forms that alumni can use to tell us of address changes and other developments in their lives. The far more commonly used medium for this information is our annual giving return envelope, which specifically asks for news that can be included in the next issue of our alumni magazine. Most alumni read their school magazines from the back forwards, beginning with the class notes, the section that is most important to them and the one section of every magazine that more or less writes itself. Our class notes section is an open forum in which we print almost verbatim the communications we receive from alumni: news about college fraternities, summer jobs, graduate degrees, work and career changes; news of engagements, weddings, births, new marriages, grandchildren, and retirements; even messages such as, ''Has anyone heard from Davis or Upchurch recently?'' The one caveat is to make sure that the news comes from the alumnus himself and not from a practical joker. A personal check inside the envelope is a good indication of authenticity.

We also involve many others in the news gathering process, taking note of phone calls and visits and off-campus encounters with alumni. This is

an excellent way to involve the faculty in the work of the alumni office
and requires only a brief annual request that the faculty keep us informed
about contacts with alumni. For our part, every time an alumnus inquires
about a teacher or sends his regards, we make sure the teacher is aware of
it. This may seem trivial, but it isn't. The bonds formed between teacher
and student are strong and sacred. For this reason we make every effort
to include current and former faculty in all alumni events both on and off
the campus; likewise, for this reason we never involve the faculty in direct
solicitation of financial support from the alumni.

The goal of this information gathering process is to keep up to date
with our alumni and, equally important, to acknowledge the events in
their lives in as personal a way as possible. I ask everyone in our office
to become involved in acknowledging alumni news and to work to become known personally to the alumni. In this regard we are fortunate in
the longevity of our alumni office personnel. I strongly believe that their
direct and personal contact with alumni adds to their job satisfaction. Gift
acknowledgement letters that we send up to the headmaster for his sig-
nature are always accompanied by the envelope bearing the alumnus'
news note for the magazine. The headmaster and others of us who sign
these computer-generated letters personalize them with postscripts that
acknowledge the news in some way.

Alumni babies receive a miniature varsity letter or a charm for a brace-
let or necklace. We often send out T-shirts and baseball caps to older
children, especially those who are nearing high-school age. When an
alumnus dies, his widow and alumni relations receive personal letters of
condolence. We recently began acknowledging birthdays with a postcard
featuring a cartoon drawn by an noted alumnus artist. The card bears a
standard greeting and a clear address label, which doesn't make it really
very personal, but, of course, it's the thought that counts. More than one
alumnus has written us to say, ''Thanks for remembering.'' We are aggressive in our fundraising efforts, but we rarely encounter that old complaint: ''I never hear from you except when you're asking for money.''

Shared experience creates the alumni community, but shared interests
give it purpose. In the former they find their sense of place. In the latter
they find their role: to help the school accomplish its mission. It is
essential that the school establish this role firmly on the high ground of
principle—service to the institution—and define the role both broadly and
clearly. No school exists to serve the personal interests of its alumni.
There should never be any suggestion of this in the school's relations with
its alumni. It is the alumni who serve the school, and in so doing their

motive must be seen as a mixture of gratitude and altruism. They are grateful for what the school has done for them, but their real interest must be to make the school better and stronger, thereby making them proud of their alma mater, of course, but on a deeper level giving them a sense of contributing to and participating in a shared effort to create a better future. A good alumni relations program must embody the same idealism the school has for its students. If we lose sight of this, our alumni community will be merely a club.

The alumni role of service to the school should be construed broadly. We must resist the natural tendency to emphasize financial contributions to the neglect or exclusion of other important avenues of service. Alumni assistance in admissions is of vital importance to the school. Properly attuned to the school's admissions program and clear about their role in it, alumni can be of invaluable help in identifying and cultivating the interest of well-qualified applicants. Most applicants and their families first learn of our schools by word-of-mouth. Most frequently that word is said by an alumnus, who can speak directly to the school's benefits. We cannot assume, however, that alumni will perform this service on their own. They must be encouraged to do so. They must also be effectively organized and adequately prepared to perform successfully their volunteer service to the school. It is highly important that they receive regular and thoughtful support from the school staff and that their efforts in behalf of the school be recognized.

For many years alumni have expressed interest in assisting our school in admissions, and there are many alumni who have made great contributions to our school in their area. Unfortunately, there are also alumni who feel that their offer to help was not heard or appreciated. Our appeal for their help was not followed with a clear and meaningful assignment, nor with direct, encouraging support from someone at the school to give them guidance and feedback. Such a frustrated volunteer called me once to say: "I offered to help. You sent me a lot of material. I haven't heard anything else from you in six months. What am I supposed to be doing?" Nothing is more corrosive to volunteer enthusiasm than a vague assignment, poor communications, or ingratitude.

Only recently we have developed an effective alumni admissions organization, complete with a name, a logo, and a well-written volunteer handbook. The key has been having adequate staff to support the organization of volunteers and to see that their efforts are properly recognized. All of our alumni admissions volunteers are now listed in a booklet that is included in the material we send to interested families, who are encouraged to contact alumni in their areas. We also notify the volunteers, who often initiate the contact, and we keep them informed throughout the admissions process. More importantly, having adequate staff support for the organization, we are able to make our volunteers proactive rather than simply reactive. A member of the admissions office staff can call alumni volunteers and give them guidance about where to find promising prospective students, how to approach them and their parents, and how to counsel them most effectively in submitting an application to our school. Our alumni volunteers are most willing to help, but without direct and regular support from the school, they can lose focus and then interest.

Alumni may also serve the school in ways that directly benefit the students. We frequently ask alumni who are prominent in their fields to address our students in assembly, in chapel, and in other forums on campus. Their remarks usually draw a strong connection between their experience at the school and their subsequent personal or professional development, living testimony to the value and reality of our school's mission. Not all alumni are good speakers, but they all approach such assignments with great seriousness and an honesty that comes from the bond they feel with the students gathered around them. From time to time we have organized a Career Day during which alumni return to school to talk with students about career possibilities and requirements. It is important that in this, as in all such alumni interaction with students, we include a broad spectrum of alumni—artists, soldiers, teachers, and ministers—and not just those who have been successful in law, medicine, and business.

We often overlook the potential for service among our youngest alumni. Recently we have started a program whereby we invite young alumni in college to return to the school to meet in small groups with juniors and seniors. The focus of their remarks is the often difficult transition to college life. Neither teacher nor parent can be as effective in such counseling as an older peer. We have also taken the initiative to go visit our alumni in college, bringing them together for lunch or dinner usually with representatives of the college also present as our guests. In this we are of course nurturing the alumni community, but we also seek to convey to our alumni our continuing interest in them and in their performance in college, which can have a positive or negative effect on the way that college views subsequent applicants from our school.

The most visible sign of a healthy alumni relations program is the alumni participation rate in annual giving. Our rate has been as high as 67%, but the ten-year average is closer to 58%. This is still comparatively high, and it reflects a constant effort on our part and on that of our volunteers to get everyone to participate. A colleague of mine used to insist that our participation rate should be 100%. He professed not to understand why an alumnus would not want to make at least a token contribution to the school each year. Although I admire this spirit and seek to instill it in our alumni volunteers, I also believe that no one is obligated to support our school.

From long experience with our alumni, I know and accept the fact that some alumni did not have a positive experience at the school. Fairly or unfairly they blame the school for things that have since happened to them, or the pattern of their lives has moved the school far away in their hearts, minds, and interests. I also know that it is virtually impossible to obtain a token contribution from them, and, frankly, trying to do so is a misuse of precious time and energy. In our office we refer to such alumni as "Stones," an acronym for those who contribute on a "Seldom-to-Never" basis. They receive from us only mailed appeals for support. We focus our fund-raising energies and our volunteers on those who are inclined to support us. The one exception is during a reunion year when we try to call everyone in the class. We never remove an alumnus from our mailing list unless he specifically requests us to do so. If he asks us to stop soliciting him, we do so, but we continue to send him all of our publications and continue to invite him to all alumni functions.

Several years ago at an alumni party in Florida, I noticed a man standing alone in a corner looking grumpy and uncomfortable—looking, in fact—like the archetypical Stone. I struck up a conversation with him and quickly got an earful about how bad things were at the school in the 1930's. Like most alumni, however, he warmed up to the subject and was soon laughing about what a stuffed shirt phony his headmaster had been. He reminded me of the way some of our students sound during the bleak doldrums of February; reminded me, in fact, of Holden Caulfield grown old. In retrospect I think his problem was that for over forty years he had been harboring what were essentially adolescent grudges against the school and against teachers long dead. A few years later he came to his 50th reunion. He still does not contribute and remains a Stone, but he and I correspond frequently. For some perverse reason I enjoy his grudge. I suspect that he does too. There must be room in the family for alumni such as these.

A good alumni relations program is not a subsidiary component of fund-raising. It is the other way around. A good alumni relations program built on a community of shared experience and interest creates the environment in which successful fund-raising takes place. Alumni don't give because we are particularly clever about asking them to do so, although we are, to be sure, persistent. They give because they are grateful for what the school means to them and because they understand and support the school's mission, which should in some way inform all of our communications with alumni. The flagship of our communications program is the school magazine, published quarterly. While the back half of the magazine is devoted to alumni news, the front half focuses on school issues and events and seeks to reveal the school's mission at work. An important feature of each magazine is the column the headmaster writes relating the school's mission and policies to issues of current significance, such as the present concern for civility. Alumni need to know that the school doesn't exist in splendid isolation, that what is going on at the school every day bears a fundamental relationship to the larger society, to that thing we so often call the real world. It is our task to make this plain.

The annual giving appeal should also clearly relate mission to the need for support and, further, should be construed as a way to enhance that mission rather than a way to moderate tuition or help pay for basic services. As a donor I want to feel that my contribution is helping provide something extra, something the school needs but may have to do without unless I pitch in to help. For most of our schools the annual giving program is presented as a way to strengthen faculty compensation, to provide scholarship assistance to students who require it, and to enhance the school's program in ways both great and small. We can and should identify these enhancements. For example, a contribution to the annual giving program can help enhance faculty salaries and produce a real increase beyond the level of inflation. Likewise, a contribution will enhance the scholarship program by helping bridge the gap between our students' needs and the income we receive from our underfunded scholarship endowment.

At the beginning of each year, furthermore, I scrutinize the school budget department by department, making a list of things a donor can buy for the school with his annual gift: computers, printers, musical instruments, desks, microscopes, lawnmowers, uniforms, maps, etc. We list these items in our annual appeal as designated gift opportunities. Not only does this list produce gifts for the school, it helps make everyone aware of the needs the school faces every year. We also publish in our school magazine a wish list of needed but currently unbudgeted items that can range from new hymnals for the chapel to a video taping system for the athletic department to large capital items like a new faculty house or a

scholarship. Again this list serves the purpose of creating greater awareness of the school's needs and often plants the seed for a significant gift
in a donor's mind.

In our contacts with alumni, we should always be prepared for that
frequently asked question: "What does the school really need?" Someone who asks this question is not thinking in terms of microscopes or
lawnmowers. He is identifying himself as a potential major gift prospect
who wants to know the larger needs of the institution. Often he has some
idea in mind, but the proper response is never, "I don't know. What do
you think?" An effective answer to this question requires an accurate,
up-to-date long-range plan for the school, a plan that looks at least five
and perhaps even ten or more years ahead. Too often we generate such
plans for our schools in advance of a capital campaign, and then promptly
lose sight of the plan as the campaign unfolds. The plan should be a living
document incorporating assumptions about the future internal and external environments and clearly identifying the institution's aspirations and
priorities. It should represent a challenging and inspiring view of the
school's future, a view that explains the need for greatly improved faculty
salaries or the need for a new science building. In our alumni development programs we should always take the long view. Present needs are
just a part of a much bolder and more inspiring vision for the school.

Our job in the alumni office is to give alumni the opportunity to
contribute to making this vision a reality. When I first heard this, I
smirked. It seems so corny to present a solicitation as an opportunity. But
now I see it as the only approach to fund-raising, an approach that dig-
nifies both the solicitor and the donor. And it depends on continually
seeking to identify the alumni's interest in a better future with the
school's mission. It means helping an alumnus find himself at the school
in the sense that his wish for a better world can take concrete form in the
education he can help provide younger people today.

At our school the year does not end with commencement but with the
Reunion Weekend, which we host on campus over the weekend following
graduation. For many years we staged class reunions in mid-May. Some
older alumni still say that they miss seeing the school in session—the
students, the games, the classes, the whole daily flow of school life that
a large, three-day event inevitably disrupts at a time when students are
completing term papers and taking Advanced Placement exams. More to
the point, however, we cannot give our alumni guests our full attention
while school is in session. By hosting the Reunion Weekend after graduation, we are able to give the alumni the run of the campus and its

athletic and dormitory facilities while giving them the undivided attention of our faculty and support staff.

In the last several years we have also adopted a modified cluster reunion format. Traditionally reunions are staged around five-year intervals ranging from the 5th to the 50th or even 60th anniversary of graduation. Although such anniversary celebrations make good calendar sense, at a four-year boarding school such as ours it means that there is no overlap among the reunion classes. None of the classes were at the school at the same time. In our modified cluster approach we hold constant the 10th, 25th, 40th, and 50th reunion anniversaries while hosting two three-class clusters around other anniversaries. For example, this spring we are hosting a 20th reunion cluster for the classes of 1973–75 and a 45th reunion cluster for the classes of 1948–50. Next year we will have 15th and 35th reunion clusters. While this approach makes it impossible to predict your next reunion without a master multi-year schedule and creates some conflicts with college reunions, it has helped make our Reunion Weekend a larger and far more attractive event for our alumni.

We have also significantly increased our investment in the Reunion Weekend, which we aim to stage in a style appropriate to our alumni's image of the school and to our sense of their importance. The food is excellent, refreshments flow freely, and the musical entertainment is enjoyable without being either loud or demanding. Typically we will have on the first evening a discjockey playing oldies or a Blue Grass band. The next night we step up the entertainment with a larger band whose range extends from Glenn Miller to the Grateful Dead. We avoid, however, having a real show. Alumni don't want or need to be entertained. They are their own entertainment, and they appreciate visiting among themselves in a relaxed atmosphere that is not too highly structured or tightly scheduled. Nor do they want to hear much about financial contributions to the school. Indeed, one imposes of their time and attention at one's peril. For this reason we keep our official program to a minimum and conduct most of it in the hour before lunch on Saturday when the headmaster speaks and responds to questions.

Our investment of time and resources goes far beyond what the participants pay in attendance fees. The attendance fee is a flat per-person charge based on one or two day's participation and includes all meals, refreshments, and activities. We also charge a token on-campus lodging fee. Current and former faculty are treated as honored guests and pay nothing. On the contrary, not only do we want them to attend, we also ask members of the faculty to run athletic events and to offer activities that may be of interest to the alumni, such as a nature walk along the river, a guided tour of nearby Civil War battlefields, or a discussion of some issue of current interest.

An activity that our alumni particularly enjoy is one in which they are asked to play the role of the director of admissions and evaluate hypothetical prospective students. This program informs the alumni about the kinds of students we seek and about the issues that come to bear in the admission process. Another activity that we have offered recently with far less success has been a financial planning seminar in support of our planned giving program. There is little interest in this during the Reunion Weekend with its emphasis on shared experiences and enduring friendships.

We find, however, that in the aftermath of a reunion, when an alumnus has had the opportunity to absorb the event and to reflect on the inexorable nature of time and change, he is often most receptive to the idea that what he gained from the school that has lasting value in his life can be preserved and made better for those who follow in his footsteps. In this way the community of shared experience merges with the community of shared interests and finds the means for renewal and growth.

8

International Students in a Day School

by David C. Burnham, Head of School
Moses Brown School

Like most day schools, Moses Brown has always had a few international students. The fact that we have a small Residential Community has, however, been especially helpful over the last nine years. Of course, I still have trouble thinking of Moses Brown as a day school. Let me explain.

Moses Brown was founded as the Friends Boarding School in New England. No day students were admitted for the first 100 years, 1784–1884. When I arrived in 1978, the boarders had dwindled to about 50, and the overall ambiance was that of a day school. The Boarding Department was looked upon as vestigial, dear to some but removed from the main life of the school.

The Board of Overseers studied the situation. Admissions was good for day students, and finding boarders of the desired academic caliber was difficult given our facilities. The Board, accordingly, decided in 1981 to phase out boarding. Then, in 1984, just as the last boarders were to leave, I persuaded our Board to allow a small residential community supervised by faculty willing to take turns cooking. Students would be expected to help clean up after meals and take care of their lounge and corridor spaces.

Since that decision was made, the Residential Community has been a success with anywhere from nine to fifteen students each year. It has helped us maintain a 24-hour show of life and lights on this city campus. It has provided some rent-free, IRS-free housing for faculty. It has enabled students whose families have moved out of town to remain and graduate, and parents have been able to tuck their children into the RC when they have taken vacations. Finally, it has made it possible for this particular day school to have a larger overseas contingent and a more diverse student body than most day schools.

I am a firm advocate of a small residential community within a day school. There are some headaches and problems and, of course, we have to be cost efficient, but the rewards are great. Our Residential Community is so small that it really does become a family with adults and young people mixing well together. We have had an English-Speaking Union exchange student at Moses Brown ever since I came here, and we have had students from many European countries and South America. We have sponsored a girl from Liberia during the last two years.

Recently there has been an influx of Asian students which has brought with it several issues. Whereas the European internationals mix fairly readily with the day student population, our students tend to keep to themselves. A plethora of Asian student candidates makes it tempting for a budget-minded headmaster to fill the RC with students from Japan, Korea, and Hong Kong. In doing so one defeats the purpose because the English-speaking boarders feel crowded out, and the Asians may spend too much time using their mother tongues.

It takes a lot of effort to keep the Residential Community from feeling isolated. This problem is exacerbated by our Asian students who usually are diligent and docile and sometimes have to be pried away from their books and rooms to mix with their peers. Our Parents' Association has helped by inviting boarders to student homes for dinner, and the faculty in the RC work hard to keep all students from just "vegging" in the lounge before the TV on weekends.

It takes constant effort on the part of the entire faculty of the school, plus a willingness not to take so many foreign students that they outnumber the residents for whom English is a first language, to make a really good Residential Community which serves the best interest of the students who live in it. By and large, I think we have done a good job at Moses Brown, and I believe that even the quietest Asian youngster can broaden the world view of his American peers and benefit a great deal from his experience at the school.

Even if a school does not have a residential community, exchange programs with host families can enrich a school immeasurably. The Russian program which we developed a few years ago with the city of Cheboksary, 350 miles east of Moscow, has proved very rewarding. Each year a group of faculty and students from Moses Brown, and other local schools, has gone to Cheboksary and been royally hosted by students and families connected with High School #4, a school where most of the classes are taught in English. Although they have sometimes had difficulty gathering the rubles, in most years the Russians have been able to send a group of students back to us, and we have tried to emulate their hospitality. Each visit is culminated by a dinner in our school dining hall. Emotions run high as young people who have become "friends for life" are about to part not knowing when they will see each other again. Memories of the Cold War are quickly softened and tears flow easily. It is a wonderful way for teenagers to learn that people are people the world over and differences are largely in systems of government and not in human hearts.

Moses Brown has just embarked upon a new venture involving Japanese students, and all the omens are good that the program will be a success. It all began a few years ago when Mr. Masaki Hitosugi of the Hitosugi Institute for Study Abroad in Numazu City, Japan began studying New England schools and came to Moses Brown. On his visits he brought with him several students who became members of the Residential Community, but he had a more elaborate plan in mind. Early in 1992, Mr. Hitosugi suggested a program which involved ten Japanese students coming to Moses Brown for a whole year and living with host families. They would all come from Toyo High School in Numazu City and would receive special English preparation. We liked the idea. So far their experience and ours has been very good, thanks to careful preparation on both sides of the Pacific. Interest in Japan, its language and culture, was built up initially by having a Japanese instructor, Toshiaki Shimamiya, here, sponsored by Mr. Hitosugi, making informal Japanese lessons available for the eighteen months prior to the arrival of our students from Japan. I appointed Tim Bickford, an energetic and knowledgeable history teacher, to be International Studies Coordinator, relieving him of one of his four regular classes. Henry Horne, Head of the Upper School, has been very supportive and has helped immeasurably with organization and planning. We appointed a Japan Committee, and through articles and assemblies we have tried to help the whole community own the program so that it is something more than the Headmaster's pet idea. Last year we completed the Multicultural Assessment Plan of NAIS. That process had a strong impact upon the community. Though its main thrust has been to make our school more receptive to people of color who reside within the United States, it certainly helped set the stage for our Japanese visitors.

To prepare the way on the Japanese side, Tim Bickford was invited to Japan last September to meet the students, their parents, and Japanese educators and officials. He had been to Japan once before, but this visit made it easier upon his return to describe the program and the students to prospective host families. His genial personality helped quell doubts in the minds of Toyo High School teachers and the parents of the boys and girls. After all, this program is quite a new, brave concept for the Japanese because the students will miss a whole year in the lock-step, test-orientated Japanese curriculum. They will return to Japan speaking good English, but their parents and many teachers worry whether the gains are worth the loss. Many Japanese are also concerned about the safety of their children in America and fear they will come back less disciplined and too independent in their thinking.

To assuage doubt and to assist the whole program, Mr. Hitosugi has sent two teachers with the ten students. One lives in the Residential Community and provides two classroom hours a day of Japanese curriculum to each student. The other is contributing to our community by giving Japanese lessons to students, faculty, parents, and overseers. Both can speak English and serve not only as a guiding Japanese presence but also as interpreters in the broadest sense of that word.

There are many keys to the success of this program but the crucial one is identifying, informing, and encouraging host families. When the program was first proposed, I took a chance that host families could be found. I knew that I could fall back on the Residential Community if not enough volunteers stepped forward. However, we did find enough families, and Tim was spectacular, visiting all potential hosts and working hard to find the best matches. He also organized three Sunday afternoon meetings with these families and with others who were willing to help by offering short visits, weekend stays, and trips to country, shore, and cities. All host families corresponded with their students ahead of time. To take the burden off the host parents and any ''brothers'' and ''sisters'' in their families, we also identified additional students, many of whom are taking Japanese lessons, to be guides and friends. All Japanese students were given faculty advisers just as in the case of regular Moses Brown students.

This March, Mr. Hitosugi invited Anne and me to Japan to meet students and parents and the faculty at Toyo High School. Everything was beautifully planned. We were given a royal welcome, and the actual signing of the agreement between the two schools was done with much ceremony, many speeches, and filmed on national television. The Mayor of Numazu City enthusiastically backed the project and invited me and the ten youngsters to his office. When I returned to Moses Brown, I was able to show videos to the host families of the various ceremonies and have them see their new family members on film. The project seems to be moving beyond the two schools, and the mayors are now talking of making Providence and Numazu sister cities.

Early April is a strange time for new students to arrive at an American school, but that is when the Japanese school year begins. Moses Brown's new students are all sixteen and beginning the middle of their three Japanese high school years. This spring they are expected to get used to the United States and to Moses Brown and to build up their skills in English. They are taking two periods of ESL, daily classes in music and art, and two hours of continued Japanese curriculum. In the summer they will stay with their host families in some cases, in others, go to boarding school ESL programs. Two teachers who run a summer camp are providing a special counseling opportunity for at least two students. The final details of the summer have yet to be worked out, but our hope is that when these boys and girls return in September we will be able to put them in the mainstream junior curriculum with some additional ESL support. Toyo High School is not asking for specific credits but only a statement of successful completion of the experience at Moses Brown.

One factor even more essential to success than the host families is the quality of the students themselves. Toyo High School has done very well by us. The young Japanese selected for the program are intelligent, flexible, polite and full of good humor. When I first saw them in Japan, they were all in uniform and practically marched during the ceremonies. I worried about how well they would adjust to the casual style of Moses Brown and the relative independence of our students. So far I think they have done well and Mr. Hitosugi, who came to visit during the first week, has only one big worry. Will the boys and girls want to go home next March?

To make this program possible, the parents of our Japanese students have been charged the regular day tuition, plus a surcharge for ESL, and a rather modest additional sum to help the host families with the cost of food. Each total payment to Moses Brown was $13,400 with the check coming in two installments from Toyo High School. Japanese parents also have to reckon on luncheon fees, transportation, books and spending money. Sending packages of clothing and other possessions ahead of time is expensive. However, these costs seem to be affordable to Toyo parents, and we intend to keep the program going year after year. My hope is that more and more Moses Brown students will take advantage of our Japanese lessons and offers from Mr. Hitosugi and Toyo High School to study in Japan.

In addition to the Japanese program, the foreign students in the Residential Community, and the Russian exchange, there are many other international students at Moses Brown. We are in a college town and often the sons or daughters of visiting professors are with us for a year. Our parents on their own sometimes sponsor students from abroad. This year we have in our day student body, young people from China, Turkey, Tibet, France, Germany, the Canary Islands, and South Africa. Then, of course, there are children from families of newly arrived immigrants from such places as Korea, Cambodia, Russia, and the Dominican Republic, just to name a few.

As most schools do, we have the usual tough financial decisions when an alumnus, parent, or friend comes in very excited about a young person from Country X whom Moses Brown could really help, but the sponsor has no money, and the school's funds have been exhausted. We simply do our best, and sometimes I get on the phone to seek a benefactor, often with success.

I believe in making our schools as open as possible to international students. We have a service which we can provide for them. But the bigger reason is to help American students learn to view the world through a larger lens. I told the Japanese students in one of my formal speeches in front of their teachers and parents that they are coming to America because my students needed them, that they were coming not just to learn but to teach. In this way one school can help draw together the pieces of this smaller, but still fragmented 21st Century world.

9

Multiculturalism

by Michael Gary, Associate Director of Admission,
Director of Multicultural Affairs
Pomfret School

Independent schools in many respects have answered the valiant call of our society to do away with segregation and to embrace the beautiful image the great Martin Luther King shared with our nation while on that mountain top, the Lincoln Memorial in Washington, D.C.: that one day little black boys and little black girls will join hands with little white boys and little white girls to sing in the great Negro spiritual, ''Free at last, free at last. Thank God Almighty, we are free at last.''

Since that day, many independent schools have developed a conscience which has dictated to them to open doors to students of color and to champion the cause of Civil Rights. As a result, today, at least in the state of Connecticut, most independent schools are more diverse than most public schools (*Hartford Courant* 2/93). Many committed independent schools have gone as far as to establish diversity goals in admissions and have allocated hundreds of thousands of dollars to their financial aid budgets to make their schools more affordable.

Our independent schools have done an impressive job in making it possible for ''little black boys and little black girls to join hands with little white boys and little white girls,'' but we have a ways to go before they begin singing that great Negro spiritual. We cannot rest on our laurels because we have just begun the process of making Martin's dream a reality. The racial tension in our schools is greater than ever, in the classroom, on the playing field, in the cafeteria and in the hallway. Political Correctness is a ''wrench'' currently slowing down the wheels of progress, causing us to become sidetracked and to take our eyes off ''the prize.'' Nevertheless, we need to be sure that we are not unwittingly barring our students of color from realizing their full academic and individual abilities because of institutional racism in our schools.

As an African-American male and Administrator at the independent school where I was one of those little black boys, I have just recently had many of my questions answered as to why race relations at our schools, not to mention our country, have not reached that next plateau. However profound, one of the reasons is lack of communication, straight talk between the students about race and between the students and faculty. Senator Bill Bradley put it best during a speech on race relations when he asked the audience rhetorically, "How long has it been since you had an honest conversation about race with someone of another race . . . If the answer is never, you're part of the problem" (*Newsweek*, May 6, 1991). We as educators do a disservice to the cause of bringing about racial harmony when we skillfully skirt issues which have to do with race, and by doing this we make it taboo to discuss such issues at our schools. We must not save our discussions about race till we read *Huckleberry Finn*, *The Color Purple*, *Their Eyes Are Watching God*, *To Kill A Mockingbird*, or until Black History Month and Martin Luther King Holiday roll around. Enough of just intellectualizing.

Our goal at Pomfret School is to make sure the channels of communication about "differences" are open and remain open. In elevating the discussion about race relations at our school, we started with one of our student organizations. Members of "Voice" rewrote the statement of purpose of "Voice," our school's multicultural organization, making its language inclusive, and changing its purpose to be a vehicle of multicultural education. Since the change to "Voice's" statement of purpose, members of "Voice" have been about the business of raising the conscience of the school community about issues pertaining to race relations. Members have written and performed their own play, portraying the struggles and triumphs of students of color at Pomfret School, and then afterwards entertained questions from their peers and members of the faculty in the audience. Since this play, the school has had at least one theatrical performance each year which deals with the issue of race relations at our school or in our country.

The organization then started a monthly student and faculty forum, where topics like "Race and Ethnicity At Pomfret," "College Admissions: Why I Got In and You Didn't," and "Police Brutality—A Black Thing?" could be discussed, allowing students and faculty members to engage in emotionally-charged discussions together. The way such a forum is managed is that we find applicable articles and distribute them, and we organize a panel of students and faculty members to present the topic of discussion, pro and con, getting the dialogue started. However, before the discussion gets started, everyone in attendance is reminded of the rules: to seek first to understand before you are understood; to avoid personal attacks; to speak only when the moderator has given you the floor.

The principle of "seek first to understand before you are understood" is explained during our new student orientation session on diversity. In doing this, we teach our new students, many of whom have never been part of a student body as diverse as ours, how to engage in a discussion about "differentness," minimizing the chance of a shouting match occurring and ultimately shutting down communication. Also, we emphasize to our new students to read the intention of others, and not just hear what is actually said. In our very first "Voice" round table discussion, it became painfully clear that many of our White-American students refrained from engaging in discussions about race with their African-American peers because of fear of making a slip and offending them. This sense of caution is not educationally sound. In fact, it is a major deterrent, making it difficult for our students to get to know their African-American peers.

Also, we help our students identify what they have in common, beyond the color of their skin, their religion, and their gender. During the summer months, new students fill out a social styles type questionnaire, and based on their social style, they are divided up into groups during the diversity session to engage in discussion around their similar social characteristics. Helping students find out what common characteristics they have enables them to establish a foundation upon which relationships are built between students of different races.

While trying to get a handle on creating an environment in which serious dialogue may occur, we are also examining every aspect of our school to assess if it is multicultural in scope and is absent of institutional racism. The Multicultural Assessment Process, a tool designed by the National Association of Independent Schools Department of Diversity, has done a wonderful job of bringing our whole community, from the Board to current parents, into the discussion about race relations at Pomfret School. The tool causes one to examine the collection of multicultural material in your school's library, the attrition rate, the racial composition of the faculty, and student life, among many other things. After a school completes its self study, NAIS' Department of Diversity sends a visiting team of trained evaluators to conduct a three day thorough examination of the school.

Our self-study revealed some interesting issues at our school, issues which might not be all too different from what is happening across the country in independent schools. Eighty percent of our faculty believes that our White-American students have many stereotypes about students of color, and that the majority of the students believe the faculty allow stereotypes to go unchallenged inside their classrooms: Our White-American students feel they are more tolerant of different races and cultures than our students of color feel they are. The one issue both the faculty and the student body overwhelmingly agree on is that they want more multicultural activity together.

What are some of the programs and activities schools are using to progress in the area of multiculturalism?

- At the Cambridge Friends School the entire board, faculty and staff have gone through anti-racism training, and new hires are expected to complete anti-racism training within one year of being hired. The school has an in-service program (Professional Development Day) where a consultant comes in to train around issues of multiculturalism.

- At the University of Chicago Lab School, its faculty supports teacher exchange programs with the Navaho High School in Grey Hills, a school in Nigeria, and a local school in Uptown, Chicago, where teachers learn firsthand about a culture different from their own. The lower school has as a part of its curriculum a program called "Treasured Holiday," where each student is asked to pick his favorite holiday and then is responsible for sharing with his classmates the importance of that holiday, making the celebration a sharing experience.

- In Minnesota, the Minnesota Minority Education Partnership (a non-profit membership organization that works closely with students,the communities of color and representatives from education, business, government and non-profits to develop programs that help students of color succeed academically) and the Minnesota Independent School Fund (a voluntary association of accredited, private secondary schools throughout Minnesota) have joined forces to create a collaborative diversity project, where parents, students, teachers, and administrators are involved with a full-time-three person staff to oversee regional diversity efforts. This collaborative effort has resulted in each school having a diversity plan, in the production of a multicultural holiday calendar, in the production of several multicultural newsletters, in a cultural field trip to Atlanta, Georgia, and in the invitation to host the Annual N.A.I.S. People of Color Conference in 1993.

- At Pomfret School issues pertaining to diversity are sometimes portrayed through theater and discussed as a community, and sometimes discussed in a roundtable format. "Race And Ethnicity At Pomfret School" was a play written and performed by "Voice" members; the "Voice" roundtable discussion titled "College Admissions: Why Did I Get In and You Did Not?" brought to the surface the realities of affirmative action and college and university attempts to recruit a more diversified group of students.

The issue of diversity is not new. The reason this topic is mentioned so much today at our schools is that never before in the history of our schools and our country have white students and students of color had the opportunity to learn together. It was just a generation ago that our country was legally segregated, and it remains so, *de facto*, in many public schools. Real dialogue between the races rarely takes place. It is for this reason we as educators must not ignore, however draining it may be, the historic opportunity we have to change by encouraging dialogue in the classroom, discussing "differentness" whether it be race, gender, religion or class.

The problem of the twentieth century is in fact the problem of the color line; but more specifically, the problem of the twentieth century is the lack of communication between the color lines and our complacency with witnessing only a little of Dr. King's dream. If we, educators and students alike, would redirect our attention towards the dream and make a commitment to engage in serious dialogue on race relations, we would be back on course, preparing that chorus to sing that great Negro spiritual, "Free at last, free at last, thank God Almighty, we are free at last."

10

Teaching Math to Girls

by Joan Countryman, Head of School
Lincoln School

Draw a picture of a teacher in a math class. Don't let lack of artistic talent impede you. What message does your drawing convey?

* * * * * * * * *

A few years ago, a young woman, an African-American freshman at a community college accepted her calculus professor's invitation to make a presentation of her work at a regional professional meeting. With the help of her teacher, she prepared a brief talk on LaGrange methods of analysis and presented the paper at the student session of the conference. She was successfully fielding questions when a male professor at the back of the room raised his hand. "Put your first transparency back on the overhead." He demanded. She obeyed and he said, "See that 6? It should be a 5."

The calculus professor, the one who told me the story, reported that her first reaction was not, "Why doesn't that jerk shut up," but instead, "how could we have missed that mistake? We worked so hard."

The end of the story is that he was wrong about the 6.

How might school mathematics change if women were central to our teaching? Would the metaphors change or would we still speak of "mastery"? Would we emphasize abstraction, and rationality, or might we choose construction and intuition? Would our concerns shift toward process and away from products? Would math still look like secrets and mysteries owned by professors with right answers? What would happen if the curriculum were more inclusive?

Gender is an issue in the mathematics classroom. Listen to the voices of some students in coed classrooms, girls and boys being taught presumably in the same circumstances.

My math career started off with a successful 9th grade year. From the very start, I enjoyed the logic behind the mathematical problems I encountered in geometry. The proofs were challenging and the problems interesting. (Boy)

For as long as I can remember, math has always been fairly easy but very frustrating for me. I have always had fairly high expectations for myself and therefore other people also expect me always to know the answer. Friends who aren't even in my math class sometimes call for help. (Girl)

In elementary school I was a very good math student and always found myself working on math level tests much higher than those of my classmates. My teachers pushed me very hard, and I often got private lessons with the teacher while the rest of the class was working on other problems. I remember being proud of being the only third-grader in the school to know long division. (Boy)

My earliest math memory is associated with failure. (In a new school) I didn't know how to multiply and the rest of the class was doing multiplication problems. I struggled to memorize the multiplication tables but I could not understand the concept of multiplication. . . . The next math memory that seems relevant is one during my seventh grade year. We began to learn algebraic equations, and I couldn't understand what the ''x'' meant in an equation like $5x+3=18$. The concept of what ''x'' stood for escaped me. I felt useless and stupid when I couldn't imagine how to solve or what to solve for in these equations. (Girl)

When teachers begin to examine questions of gender and mathematics they notice that:

- standardized testing shows that girls start school ahead of boys in computation.
- by the time they graduate from high school, boys have higher math SATs.
- high school girls still seem less committed to careers, more interested in marriage or stereotypically female jobs.
- girls are less likely to take math and science even when they show ability in those areas.

- girls are more likely to believe they are incapable of doing math and science and to avoid it in high school and college.
- girls attribute failure to lack of ability and success to luck.
- boys attribute success to ability and failure to bad luck.

Twenty-five years ago, when I started teaching high school math in a coed school, there were few female students enrolled in advanced mathematics and science courses. I don't recall any discussion of gender in those days. We cared about teaching and learning to be sure, but when we spoke of standards of excellence we were simply proud of any students who attained high levels of achievement. Most academic awards in science and math went to boys, in language and literature to girls.

Then concern about the lack of achievement among girls began to emerge as a national issue. First, some researchers argued that there was a genetic basis for superior male achievement in mathematics. Next, in response, we heard that something was wrong with the teaching of women. Teachers were advised to encourage female students who were handicapped, anxious or poorly motivated, presumably because they were female.

I began to wonder about this problem of women and mathematics. Was there something wrong with women, or was there something wrong with mathematics? Did girls perform less well than boys? At all grade levels? In all circumstances? On all tasks? How wide was the gap between female and male performance at the secondary level? How should a teacher respond to those differences? What could you say to girls who insisted that their right answers were ''lucky''? How did you answer the mothers who explained that they ''never could do math either''?

Peggy McIntosh's challenge in ''Phase Theory of Curriculum Reform''[1] led me to examine the core of my discipline. How would mathematics have to change to reflect the fact that women are the majority of the world's population? Would the woman-less, white male mathematics that we were teaching (McIntosh's phase one) disappear? Might we go beyond injecting a few women into the curriculum (phase two)? Already I had seen that while discussing famous women mathematicians motivated a few students, the models of excellence were still white and male.

Women are seen as victims in the stage McIntosh calls phase three. Why don't girls win the math contests? Why are there no pictures of women in the textbooks? Who decides that the word problems talk about sports? Sexism (and racism) are topics of study, but women (and other excluded groups) become ''the problem.'' It is a depressing phase. ''Who deserves more pity," students ask as they compete for underdog status. "Men, (women), blacks (whites) are victims, too," they complain.

In phases four and five, McIntosh challenges us to use women's experiences as the lens through which we view the world. It engages emotion and rationality. We move away from examining oppression toward examining privilege, revealing how the structure affects everyone, not just the victims. We raise new questions, and make new assumptions. We study not just others, but ourselves. We begin to tell our stories, and listen to the life histories of others. It is the stage of mathematics autobiographies, and stories like Sonia Sanchez' "Norma."[2] What can we learn about math and science from reflecting on our own experience?

The mathematics reform efforts generated by the *Curriculum and Evaluation Standards* published five years ago by the National Council of Teachers of Mathematics[3] provide some answers. Writing to learn, real-world applications, mathematical modelling, collaborative group work, and mathematics as communication are just a few of the host of new approaches to teaching and learning mathematics that reformers are advocating. Supported by extraordinary new technology this new "new mathematics" is consistently richer and deeper than the reforms of the 1960s and 1970s.

Change will not come overnight, however, in a world where parents have lower expectations for daughters than for sons and are more willing to accept low levels of achievement in math from girls. Teachers will need to give up seeing math as a male domain, and learn to pay attention to girls in their classrooms. Students will have to change their beliefs about math as well.

Right now more than twenty million children study mathematics in elementary and secondary school in the United States. Most of their time is devoted to computation, practicing tasks that hand calculators can do faster and more efficiently. If you ask those children to tell you what it means to do mathematics they will say, "add, subtract, multiply, divide." As they get older many of those children will say that they hate mathematics.

Chances are that the math teacher that I asked you to draw looked like a prim schoolmarm or an absent-minded professor standing at a blackboard in front of rows and desks. When that image fades, when the teacher in the math class looks less like a "sage on the stage" and more like a coach or a "guide on the side," more of our children, the girls and the boys, will find mathematics compelling. An inclusive curriculum will help bring us there.

NOTES

1. Center for Research on Women, Wellesley, MA.
2. Sonia Sanchez. *homegirls & handgrenades*, New York, Thunder Mouth Press. 1984.
3. NCTM, *Curriculum and Evaluation Standards*. Reston, VA NCTM. 1989.

11

The Hiring & Firing of Faculty

by Clinton P. Wilkins, Head of School
College Preparatory School

The hiring of faculty is the single most important role a school head plays. This is a strong statement indeed, especially in light of the many functions a head serves as well as the multiple, competing constituencies he or she addresses. Yet if you believe, as I do, that teachers are at the heart of a school and that the relationships between teachers and students are the very soul of schooling, then this statement takes on special meaning. It is in this context that hiring becomes the pivotal moment in the cycle of the school year, a brief yet profound window of opportunity to strengthen a school and improve the lives of the students. In addition, and perhaps as critical, the manner in which the process of hiring is carried out becomes emblematic of the head's leadership.

Hiring decisions, in the aggregate, also signal the direction the school is moving and give shape to the head's vision as well as personality to the head's values. Hiring decisions, over time, set a lasting tone for what Seymour Sarason has called the "routines of schooling." In most independent schools, teachers are inextricably tied into these routines of school life. They participate in decision-making, particularly in matters of curriculum. They are active in the many committees which allow a school to function. They work with each other in countless ways, from team teaching to covering each others' classes. And they are central to the maintenance of standards and sound discipline. The qualities teachers bring to their endeavors are inestimable, requiring of them maturity, restraint and sound judgment.

To underscore this point, one needs only to cite the all-too-common deviations from this ideal in virtually every school, deviations which tear at the very fabric of the school culture. Some examples: one teacher may view his or her role as the promoting of a particular political agenda; another may look to the school as a therapeutic community, seeking self-esteem inappropriately through the affirmation and adulation of students; still another may be on a moral crusade to demonize those in positions of authority and power. We have all seen these forces in action. Thus, to minimize these deviations from the ideal and to embrace the qualities we desire, the process of hiring needs to be thorough, deliberate, painstaking and, yes participatory. As the old saying goes, "A stitch in time saves nine."

This essay will focus on my own somewhat idiosyncratic list of qualities I seek in teachers and the search process I utilize—from the gathering of names and resumes to the actual decision. I will also add a few caveats where appropriate. Undoubtedly your situation will differ somewhat, yet most of these ideas (none of which is new) should prove applicable. One of the most positive and creative features of independent education—and in the long run so renewing—is that there are no cookie-cutter, mechanical lists for anything we do; everything is contextual.

Qualities of Teachers

My own list of qualities which institute good teaching begins with a teacher's background. I look for a person who has a genuine and palpable love of learning, a solid knowledge base in his or her field and a demonstrated enjoyment of rigorous academic training. From this base I look for other academic and intellectual qualities: a healthy respect for proper English usage; well-versed and well-read in a variety of fields; intellectual playfulness and open-mindedness. Advanced degrees may, or may not, embody these qualities. A doctorate both piques my interest and engenders skepticism: the commitment and rigor are noteworthy, but the degree of specialization can be a true liability in working with young people.

The next level of qualities on my hierarchical scheme involve teaching skills: especially the ability to communicate with young people as well as natural ease in their company; warmth; humor; and accessibility. I look for a spark and a sense of vitality as well as stamina, perseverance and a willingness to put in long hours, whether in preparation for class or in correcting written work. A good teacher also has to "play hurt" on occasion. If a teacher embodies these qualities, combined with the courage to hold students to high academic and personal standards, he or she is bound to be both stimulating and effective. In brief, such a teacher will motivate students and help them to unlock unrecognized potential.

Finally, and most crucial, I look for the most elementary and basic human qualities: integrity; respect for others; responsibility. If these qualities are manifest, then a teacher—whatever his or her flaws or eccentricities—is bound to become a contributing member of the community, a supportive colleague and a natural "moral example" (to use Richard Rodriguez's apt phrase) for young people to emulate.

The Search Process

With these qualities in mind, let us enter into the search process itself, which is designed to locate and assess people who reflect these ideals. The process needs to be thorough enough to identify a reasonable number of qualified people, exclusive enough and timely enough so that opportunities, when presented, are not squandered. This all requires organization, teamwork and a readiness to act at the propitious moment. What follows are the major steps.

Getting the Word Out, Gathering Names and Resumes

Use a variety of means to disseminate an opening. Teacher placement agencies are often helpful, although the downside is that they usually require considerable screening. Professional contacts are useful, whether they are colleagues in other schools, in universities or career placement offices. Friends of the school, alumni, and current faculty are excellent sources, since they know the school culture so well. I also still advertise, depending of course on the supply of talent. *Education Week* or local newspapers can yield results. In searching for people of color, I will contact agencies such as ABC (A Better Chance), local organizations (such as the Multicultural Alliance in my region, the Bay Area), or friends and alumni. I also do not overlook another source—those unsolicited (but not generic) letters which come in over the transom. Whatever the source, I try to spread the net widely and not overlook any, single category.

Screening Applicants

Once I have begun to assemble a file of applicants, I make sure that the assistant head (or the academic dean) and the department head screen the viable candidates from the also-rans. Timeliness is essential here, especially since the most attractive candidates are in the most demand. As a result, I try to schedule regular meetings with the search team to monitor progress and arrange for visits.

The Visit

If the person is local, he or she may meet only with the academic dean and the department head as a preliminary step. If the person is from out of town, then a few references are checked and the visit is arranged. The visit should include a tour of the facilities, interviews with the search team (as a group and/or individually), the teaching of a sample class and informal time (such as lunch) to meet with members of the department. Each of these exercises is important; taken together they usually give me the information and perspective and the interactive feel I need to form a substantive judgment. Immediate feedback from the team is crucial.

The Interview

In the interview I try to check out the qualities I value most (see aforementioned qualities) and ascertain whether the applicant will be a creative fit with the school culture. I probe for breadth and depth of knowledge, for vitality and that special spark, and for any potential danger signals such as rigidly held views, special unexpressed needs or evidence of interpersonal conflict. In short, I am interested in a mature person (whether it is a rookie or a veteran) who is interested primarily in teaching, not in remaking the world, or the school, in his or her own image. I go into the interview with no mechanistic or preordained list of questions. Nor do I employ a particular method. I try to make the candidate as comfortable as possible, giving him or her a clear sense of me and the school. After all, once an offer is made, it is ultimately the candidate's decision!

Observation of Teaching

I have come to value the observation of a sample class as an invaluable analytic tool. I often leave this function to the academic dean and the department head, who are better positioned to evaluate the basic mechanics of teaching (such as preparation, organization, pacing and classroom management), as well as tone and the quality of relationships with students. The observation of a sample class yields much information, and uncovers the critical intangibles so necessary for success.

Comparing Impressions

After a candidate has negotiated all the steps, I like to meet with the search team to compare observations and draw conclusions. Often the formal meeting is scheduled after all the finalists have made their visits; but informal feedback is both immediate and natural as each candidate comes through. At this stage, I am careful to let the team know that their perspective is respected and valued. But I am equally careful to let them know that I have further work to do: ie, the checking of confidential references from current and previous employers or supervisors; and, in reconciling other interests outside the team's purview, such as out-of-class activities (coaching, advising, etc.) or budgeting concerns. Ultimately, it is the head's decision, for which he or she, bears the ultimate responsibility. While consensus is a noble ideal it is not always either necessary or advisable.

In the final analysis the hiring of faculty is a matter of trust. Does our school community entrust its young people to adults who will operate on a daily basis in the relative isolation of the classroom and out of full administrative view? Do the head and his or her colleagues have the confidence that the new teacher will grow and develop to meet the ever-changing demands of our times? Does the head have the faith that the new teacher will help bring the school community closer to its ideals and mission? It is in this context that the hiring process becomes the most critical function a school head can perform.

The Dismissal of Faculty

One of the most difficult and least pleasant of all administrative tasks is the termination of an employee, particularly a teacher. Whether it is an immediate and sudden departure or a slow process spanning a year or more, termination requires the utmost care, sensitivity and yes, humanity on the part of a school head. It is not my intention to catalogue every case or contingency—for this would fill volumes—but to lay out some common sense advice which may guide the reader through potentially rocky shoals.

To embark on this journey I propose a conceptual framework which includes five components. The first involves the school's faculty and staff handbook. This becomes a head's contractual and procedural guide, the basis upon which all action emanates. The second involves types of departures, ie, precipitous or slow. The third involves the stage of a teacher's career, especially the new or rookie, the veteran at mid-career, and the teacher approaching retirement. The fourth component consists of administrative actions, with an emphasis on process as well as fairness. And the fifth component consists of the core school values which are embodied for better or for worse, intentionally or not, publicly or privately—in a particular departure. These values are powerful to say the least, and they can be either one's most useful friend or one's most troublesome adversary.

Each component is a useful analytic tool, to be sure, but it is in the interplay between and among these five components which makes this framework potentially relevant for nearly every case. By necessity these five components are laid out in a linear, serial fashion. However, it is best to think of them as working simultaneously and in concert.

The Handbook for Faculty and Staff

Buttressing any administrative action is the handbook, which should be reviewed annually by a lawyer to ensure that it is thorough, current, and internally consistent. The handbook functions in two critical ways involving the dismissal of an employee. First, as an extension of the contract, all parts must be observed. Second, the handbook should spell out in detail the evaluation system itself, emphasizing various classifications of status and stages in career development. If the handbook is clear and efficient in these two areas, most contingencies should be covered.

Types of Departures

The Sudden Departure

The sudden, precipitous departure is often among the least ambiguous decisions a school head makes. Fortunately it is a relatively rare occurrence, usually involving an act so egregious that the head is left with no other recourse. What becomes critical, however, is the means in which the departure is effected.

Before a final decision is made, it is important to involve legal counsel early on in the process. An attorney well-schooled in labor law is particularly useful in reviewing the case and giving the head much needed perspective. This is especially true in the balancing of the employee's rights—particularly when it involves reputation and future employability—with the health and integrity of the institution. Once the decision has been reached, the continued assistance of legal counsel is advisable, communication with relevant board members is essential and political sensitivity is critical.

Sudden departures most often preclude any public accounting of the episode and as such can become a potential matter of mistrust between and among the faculty, parents, administration and the Board. This is why any action taken, however private, must conform not only with the letter of the law, but also with the spirit of the school's most deeply held moral values. This is why it is imperative for the administration to go to extreme ends to be fair to all parties involved. In the absence of any public statement, it falls upon those few in the know to exercise damage control by supporting the decision without, of course, breaching confidentiality.

The "Routine" Departure
Just as disruptive, but perhaps even more nettlesome is the departure which takes time, potentially a full school year or more. Usually this is a teacher who is a mixture of qualities, who may be adequate in some areas but inadequate in others, who may be serving the needs of some students but failing with others, a teacher who may engender passionate support in some quarters of the community and often hostility in other quarters. If the handbook is clear on procedures for formal faculty evaluation, especially at key career stages, then such thorny problems can become closer to a matter of routine. If the handbook is not, with regard to either evaluation procedures or to career stages, then the administrator is left in uncharted waters, battling dangerous and competing crosscurrents.

Stages in Teachers' Careers

It is important to acknowledge and emphasize that teachers are, and should be, treated differently depending upon their age, experience in the field and years of service to the school. For the purpose of this exercise they fall into three categories: the "new" teacher, who has only a few years of experience; the veteran, who may be at mid-career; and the teacher who is nearing retirement.

For the new teacher, it is expected that there will be intensive evaluation in the first few years. As a result, his or her suitability to either the school or to the profession should become clear. So the "dismissal" of such a teacher merely becomes a matter of not renewing a one-year contract. What becomes more difficult, however, is the veteran teacher who has lost effectiveness or the older teacher, approaching retirement, who may no longer be meeting the needs of the current generation of students. There are no easy answers to the latter two cases, but if all the components of this framework are observed, then the process becomes more fair for everyone.

Administrative Actions

This subject has been addressed obliquely under the rubric of sudden departures. When one is contemplating a more routine departure, however, it is equally important to observe an intentional and logical method. I offer a few salient words of advice.

Once a school head has come to the conclusion that there is ample reason to dismiss a teacher, then the concerns should be communicated directly to the teacher, in person and in the presence of either or both the academic dean and department head. This meeting should be followed by a letter, cataloging the concerns, articulating a date by which these concerns need to be addressed, and offering assistance, including a timetable for regular and periodic meetings to monitor progress. Once the target date has been reached, it is essential to hold a final session in order to determine the appropriate course of action. If the progress has been mixed, and more time is needed, merely repeat the procedure. If a decision is clear, and dismissal in order, then any actions are supported by a fair and compassionate process. There is also a paper trail.

A few caveats: Always give the teacher the opportunity to respond and improve. Don't do anything irrational, precipitous or capricious. Make sure you have lived up to your word. Bring in legal counsel. And again, leave a paper trail.

Hiring and firing—these two most time consuming and difficult tasks—are at the very crux of good schooling, especially if you believe, as I do, that the relationship between teacher and student is the pivotal concept in one's formal education. The time and care put into both hiring and firing decisions are emblematic of a head's vision. Individually, these decisions can directly benefit countless students almost immediately; in the aggregate these decisions, over time, give shape and humanity to the very future of the institution itself.

12

Rookie Teachers in Independent Schools

by Ruth Huyler Glass, Upper School Head,
The Langley School &
Richard Barbieri, Executive Director, AISNE

Brinley Hall's head, Marianne Davis, stepped to the podium to open the year's first faculty meeting. "I'd like to begin by introducing four new members of our staff. Alice Stebbins comes to us from Dartmouth, where she majored in classics and rowed on the women's crew. Oscar Nieto completed his bachelor's degree in English at Berkeley, then spent a year on a fellowship at Cambridge University in England. Denise Tidwell comes to the science department after two years with Meade Laboratories, whose staff she joined after graduation from the University of Vermont. And Lance Morehead will be teaching history after four years of honors work in East European studies at Harvard, and a career on the school's squash team that resulted in two personal and three team Ivy League championships. I know they're all going to be great assets to Brinley's faculty, and I trust you all to make them feel a part of our team."

Six months later, Marianne is meeting with her upper school division head and her dean of faculty. "Well, it looks as if we're not doing as well as we expected with our rookie teachers. Lance has decided to apply for the Foreign Service; he says the range of American, ancient, and modern European history is just too much for him and maybe he isn't cut out for high school teaching. Tom Slaughter says he thinks he can work with Denise in biology, but next year will be a test of whether she can learn to get the IPS material across to ninth-graders. Oscar seems to be doing okay after all those parent complaints about his workload and his severe grading policy. And Alice thinks she'd like to do a doctorate in Greek archeology; she told me last week that sweating under the Cretan sun will seem easy after her course, advising, and coaching load. Oh well, I suppose we have to expect years like this once in a while.''

Such oft-told tales suggest both the strength and the weakness of independent schools' methods of hiring and handling new teachers. Like many schools, Brinley Hall (an imaginary but representative institution) prides itself on hiring the brightest and the best of liberal arts graduates. Rejecting the ''Ed school'' approach, the school believes that subject area knowledge is more important than methodology courses or student teaching experience, and accordingly hires the vast majority of its new teachers straight from the ranks of arts and science majors. New teachers are given their course assignments and other duties by the relevant deans and division heads. After a week of opening faculty meetings they are left pretty much on their own to teach the syllabus developed for their courses by the department, or in some cases created by themselves after a June conference with their new department heads. The results are all too often like those described above. Yet independent schools continue to attract capable teachers year after year, and also to receive enthusiastic reviews from students and families for the quality of their teaching.

How can this be? On the one hand, independent schools long ago grasped a very important truth: you can't teach what you don't know. During the 1980s the mountains of government and foundation reports on public education came to the dismaying conclusion that teacher preparation in the public sector was woefully inadequate, turning out teachers who could not pass basic competency exams and whose subject area knowledge was out of date or superficial. Throughout the country, new programs began, most of which are just now coming to fruition, which required beginning teachers to have a subject major and in other ways to demonstrate that they knew enough history, math, science, or language to teach the discipline for which they were being certified. Independent schools patted themselves on the back and said, ''See, we had it right all along.''

But as a sage once said, the opposite of a profound truth is another profound truth. Just as you can't teach what you don't know, you also can't teach what you don't know how to teach. We have all known the superlative athlete, cook, dancer, or sailor who can perform their art beautifully, but who is simply hopeless at conveying their knowledge to others. For lack of patience, understanding of the point of view of the novice, or simple skills of exposition, the best practitioners often fail as teachers. So it is with the academic disciplines as well. Young teachers who love their subjects may often be able to convey that love, but they can be greatly assisted by some knowledge of adolescent behavior, age-appropriate reasoning skills, and at least the rudiments of a vocabulary of learning styles. Schools which take on rookie teachers who have no classroom experience and no background in methods of teaching often suffer the same results as schools which depend entirely on state certification for credentialing: they see their young teachers crash into obstacle after obstacle, quickly becoming discouraged and deciding to leave the profession before either side has given the other a fair chance.

Effective programs for incorporating rookie teachers—those which develop faculty most inclined to remain in teaching—start within each school. Good schools begin their training of rookies during initial interviews. They make a point of describing accurately the time and energy demands necessary for effective teaching. When candidates visit on campus, administrators provide opportunities for them to meet and talk with faculty members in various stages of teaching. They encourage prospective teachers to ask questions, and they outline the demands of a normal school year. It's easy, as an administrator, to be lulled by a candidate's enthusiasm and willingness to commit to almost anything. We have learned by experience, for example, that a person desirous of a job will cheerfully avow a great love of camping—until it comes time the next spring for the primitive, four-day backpack. At that point he redefines the "love" as limited to Winnebagos in national park campgrounds. Similarly, addressing the realities of a social life is a necessity. Boarding schools have a sort of advantage, if they hire a number of rookies, in that everyone is in the same boat. Experience suggests that the demands of a teaching schedule are not something that friends in other fields necessarily understand or appreciate. It's difficult to explain that papers simply must be graded and lessons prepared, and that there is no option to go out on a moment's notice.

Many schools use a mentor system to assimilate new teachers. It is critical to choose mentors carefully, not only for their competence within their own classrooms, but also for their time management and ability to communicate. If possible, a teacher who mentors should have time to do so built into his or her schedule. The same is true for the rookie. Unfortunately, many schools capitalize on the energy and inexperience of the rookie, overscheduling the unsuspecting soul. No rookie should be expected to coach a sport every season. New teachers should have time built into their schedules to work with more experienced teachers, to observe various classes. A good mentor system provides time for the two teachers to work together and clearly defines the responsibilities of one to the other. While it is not essential that a mentor be in the same department as the rookie, it can be helpful. Having a department chair or a division head serve as a mentor ensures that the curriculum will be covered adequately and at a proper pace. If sections of the same class are taught by more than one teacher, assign the more experienced teacher as a mentor, if it is at all possible. That way students in each class (and their parents) are assured of parallel syllabi.

Some schools have found it beneficial to schedule regular meetings with rookies. One school we know developed a program for all teachers new to the school, requiring that they meet weekly with the head of the school as a group. The advantage to this system was that, while the group was small enough to be extremely interactive, it included teachers both new to teaching and those with some considerable experience in other schools. The needs of the established faculty in terms of becoming familiar with their new school were met, even while they were able to share their expertise with the rookies. In fact, the meetings were so positive, productive, and popular, that the rest of the faculty insisted they be included. In the end, the head held breakfast meetings once a week that were open to all faculty members (K-12), and in which he used the time to address a wide range of philosophical questions. The experienced faculty were quite willing to share their professional development with the rookies, and a number of informal mentor partnerships developed.

Formal professional development programs are an essential part of any good school, and as much money as the budget allows should be set aside for in-service training, as well as to send faculty off campus. Rookies often need to be persuaded of the value of attending appropriate workshops. Caught up in the overwhelming cycle of the first year of teaching, it is difficult for them to appreciate that the effort it will take to prepare for classes in advance and then make up for missed work when they return will be worth it. To that end, rookie support groups are invaluable. If possible, send two rookies to a workshop together—or one rookie and a mentor teacher. As with our students, it's critical to model an attitude toward learning among adults.

Administrative supervisors should meet regularly with rookie teachers and become familiar with their teaching styles. Often the most important role the administrator plays is to listen, acknowledging that there is simply too much for the rookie to absorb all at once. One division head we know was amused recently when she and a rookie teacher agreed it would be helpful for her to sit in on a class that was giving him some trouble.

On her recommendation, the rookie asked his students for some specific feedback on how he might make the class better. Because he asked, they were respectful. They also gave him about ten very clear suggestions—all of which his administrator thought she had taught him at the beginning of the year. She was reminded that, much like the students in his class, he couldn't possibly learn everything at once. She did write down the students' suggestions and give them to the rookie, however, and he was much better able to understand their value at that point. A plus in the process was that, in explaining how he might be better, this man's students clearly demonstrated that they had learned a great deal from him.

Schools which have the budgets to do so should take advantage of the growing number of new teacher institutes sponsored by various independent school associations around the country. Fall workshops generally run from a Sunday afternoon through a Tuesday. They include a variety of elements, depending on the history and location, and whether they serve elementary, secondary, or K-12 teachers. But they share some common qualities. All try to balance the affective and the intellectual, with sessions focusing on "how's it going?" as well as specific units on subject matter, discipline, and the like. Videotaping a classroom segment is usually the climactic event of the three days.

An advantage of the fall, new teacher workshop is that it speaks to an involved—sometimes desperate—audience. By allowing new teachers a three-day hiatus after five weeks' teaching, and giving them ample time to talk with each other and with experienced professionals, the fall workshop allows for free-flowing and open discussion of the paramount problems encountered by the participants. These range from general feelings of being overwhelmed to specific concerns about dealing with rebellious students, handling a range of abilities in a single classroom, or coping with the attacks of a difficult parent or the uncooperativeness of a senior colleague. Many young teachers have told us that the workshop came at "just the right time" and was "a lifesaver." Schools which do not have access to a fall workshop need to find similar ways to allow young teachers to share their early experiences and get advice and support in a safe setting.

Other programs have been developed which require the rookie's participation in a week-long immersion during the latter part of the summer designed to provide him or her with as much preparation as possible for those opening days and weeks of school. Three such programs of which we are aware are the New Teacher Institute (Virginia Association of Independent Schools), the New Teacher Seminar (Connecticut Association of Independent Schools and Independent Schools Association of Massachusetts) and The Beginning Teacher Institute (Independent Schools Association of the Central States).'' At each site, under the supervision and instruction of several master teachers, forty or so rookies gather. For six days they prepare syllabi and lesson plans, are videotaped during a class presentation, learn to write effective comments, explore issues of adolescence and gender, and role play every difficult interaction they might conceivably have with parents, recalcitrant students, inflexible teachers, pushy board members. They learn different teaching strategies, how to set up a grade book, what the skeleton of a school year looks like from the teacher's vantage point. As important as anything else, they are forced to be awake and attentive by 7:30 in the morning and required to work until late at night preparing their assignments for the following day. In short, they have their first taste of ''real life''—their lives in their schools, not in college where they often have had the option of selecting courses according to the times they are offered (generally, we gather, not until after noon). As important as anything else, the rookies have the opportunity for a constant dialogue with others who share their questions and fears, as well as with experienced teachers. This exchange is beneficial in itself.

It has been noted that, for those college students or recent graduates interested in teaching as a career, their choice is at best ignored and at worst challenged by their peers who are more interested in making money. New teachers need to have their career choices validated. The values of the new teacher seminars, whether they be of the weekend or week variety, are many. Certainly a primary one, however, is the chance for both rookies and master teachers to have their avocations confirmed by each other. A rookie of five years ago, still in teaching and committed to remaining so, put it this way:

> I'd have to say that looking back I found NTI the first place I'd ever felt so comfortable with people—people who value ideas as precious commodities, nuggets of information to be traded and shared. Quite simply, my stay at NTI was the first time I found myself surrounded by a group of people who placed a similar respect and emphasis on the importance of education. Even at Princeton, where I must believe that undergraduates prize higher education, I never felt wholly comfortable discussing with my peers my (or anybody's) future as a teacher in (secondary school) education. While I may have believed (and still do!) in the importance of teaching, I rarely sensed that the person with

whom I was speaking fully understood my beliefs or shared the power of my conviction. Remember, most of my classmates were swept away by the Wall Street Blob—the ever-expanding indistinguishable mass of glut, greed, and (self-) gratification; a position in education simply didn't (and doesn't) jive with BMW, Bermuda, and Banking.

The NTI faculty and students comprised a small community in which the give and take of ideas and information was truly equal. I try not to imagine how rough the first few months of school would have been my first year if I had not attended NTI. Throughout that first year I continually replayed in my mind my experiences—the lectures, role plays, and in-between moments—at NTI as I did my best to navigate the "routine" (whoever coined that word, anyway?) educational waters of secondary school.

(Jay Wood, NTI III)

We have concentrated on the first year of teaching in this essay, and even on the first months of that year. But this is not to suggest that the teaching journey ends with a good first step. One young teacher who was part of an outstanding independent school teaching fellows program, which offered weekly seminars, departmental mentors, and a slightly reduced teaching load in the first year, observed, "My first year I really felt like something special. Now that I'm in my second year and just a teacher, my colleagues feel freer to be petty with me." Throughout the first few years of teaching, young teachers need frequent feedback and encouragement, opportunities to refine their skills through attendance at conferences and workshops, and an effective evaluation procedure. Support for teachers can never end, as the next chapter amply demonstrates. To close with one last truth, those who never stop learning make the best teachers.

13

The Best Is Yet To Be: Nurturing the Experienced Teacher

by Richard Barbieri, Executive Director, AISNE &
Nancy Russell, Lower School Head, Nansemond-Suffolk Academy

Greg is fifty years old. He has been teaching history at his school for seventeen years of a twenty-two year career and has no plans for moving or for career advancement. "I agreed to be department chair for two years when nobody else would do it, but I hated it, so I went to someone else and told her she had to do it. She's better at it than I was, and she's been doing it ever since."

So is Greg still growing as a teacher? Last year a researcher from the college where he was enrolled for a Master of Arts in teaching drew Greg's name at random and asked to observe some classes. His comment after three visits: "You have a willingness to be flexible, to try new ways of teaching old material, and to try new material as well, that I've hardly ever seen in a teacher your age." This year a younger observer, studying the school as part of his degree work, said to Greg, "You don't lecture — you're the only one I've seen here who doesn't lecture." In the past three years Greg:

- was highlighted on community cable TV for his cooperative teaching methods as his ninth-grade geography students role-played a crisis in an Israeli Druze village;
- added a new curriculum in Mapping the World by Heart to the geography program;
- developed a multicultural history and literature course with his department chair;

- worked on a new English-social studies interdisciplinary program;
- undertook a major revision of the middle school curriculum in concert with another teacher;
- offered to be the first to experiment with mixed-ability grouping instead of the school's traditional tracked approach.

There are two questions we need to ask about Greg: in what ways is his school responsible for his creativity and energy, and why aren't there more Gregs in our schools?

The answer to the first is fairly easy. Much of Greg's liveliness is inborn: he began his working life as a chef, then switched to teaching, first in mathematics, then in social studies, first in a big city, and now in a rural area. (Three years ago he took a leave of absence to open his own restaurant. Fortunately for his students, the economy wasn't right for his enterprise and he brought his enthusiasm back to the school.) Greg's work is also part of a full and rounded life. He is married to a kindergarten teacher and together they watch students progress from her class to his after eight to twelve years. They are ''pillars of the community,'' with a wide range of friends and hobbies—fishing and boating for him, painting and gardening for her—and with two successful daughters.

But his school plays a role too. Over the past three years Greg has had five professional development grants, some to attend extended curriculum workshops, others to work independently. The school paid for part of his master's degree as well. Further, his administration is willing, insofar as budgets allow, to let him and his colleagues build new courses and try them out. Finally, the community gives him extensive recognition: last spring his whole family was profiled in the town paper as all four members received degrees at once—a high school diploma, a B.F.A., and two masters in education.

Unfortunately, Greg says it's easy for him to get grant funds, since fewer than 15% of the faculty normally apply for them. Those who observe his classes take pains not only to praise him, but to point out how rare a phenomenon he is. This leads us to the most important question: how can our schools ensure that most of their experienced teachers are more like Greg?

That there aren't enough Gregs, even in independent schools, is beyond question. Our schools may be filled with energetic, able teachers, but how often do we hear phrases like ''burn-out,'' ''on-the-job retirement,'' or ''he hasn't had twenty years' experience, just one year's experience twenty times'' to describe teachers who are no longer excited or exciting?

Studies show that teachers do most of their growing in the early years of their career, and that few teachers are doing a better job in their fifteenth year than in their fifth.

The reasons for stagnation are several. Some are found in the conditions of the typical classroom, others in those of the typical school, while still others are societal or simply part of the life process. One concerned critic described the state of the typical teacher in the closed classroom as one of "isolation, degeneration, and stress." Without regular observation by other professionals, teachers tend to stick to the same routine year after year, with no way of measuring how effective they are being or how well other approaches might work. Schools often exacerbate this tendency, since freeing time for teachers to watch other teachers costs money, and most schools are satisfied as long as a teacher is adequately filling the same slot he or she has always filled, or better yet, is willing to plug whatever gaps need plugging this September, without asking whether the teacher is growing or stagnating.

Another cause of stagnation is the sameness of the teacher's life, year in and year out. In other professions, one can rise within the field: from lieutenant to general, from intern to chief of surgery, from attache to deputy ambassador, from associate to partner, from lecturer to full professor. Only elementary and secondary teaching has neither titles nor changes of responsibility (other than perhaps getting more of the "best" classes) as evidence of growth and maturity in your chosen field. Again and again teachers lament that the only way to get ahead is to leave the classroom. Candidates for deanships or division headships almost always begin by professing their love of the classroom and their regret at leaving it, but the desire for personal growth, recognition, increased influence, and of course enhanced income, drive many lovers of the classroom out before they have fully satisfied that love and reached their potential.

Finally, not enough schools seem to recognize that as teachers age, their life concerns change and personal issues affect their attitude toward work. To paraphrase the old aphorism about little children and big children, young teachers by and large have little problems; older teachers have big problems. Issues of aging and health, growing children, college tuitions, buying a home, caring for elderly parents, or simply wondering whether their lives are going where they had hoped, often take up enormous stores of time and energy for the thirty-something to sixty-something teacher. Schools can do little to affect these normal passages of life, but they can at least acknowledge that being constantly around the young and being constantly young are not at all the same thing. (Indeed, the saddest of aging teachers are those who never recognize this fact for themselves.) And where the issue is directly connected to the exigencies of a teaching life, there is much a responsive administration can do.

Most dilemmas faced by mid-career and veteran teachers are similar. Teachers participating in an experienced teacher seminar each of the last five years repeatedly listed these concerns among others:

- The continued expansion of teachers' responsibilities;
- Insufficient time in the day to get things accomplished at home and at school;
- The need to age gracefully;
- The lack of financial security;
- An inability to keep up with the vast changes in techniques, technology and curriculum;
- The desire to be counted as a vital member of a young faculty;
- The difficulty of career path decisions.

While we cannot lengthen the day in order to allow teachers to fit in more, nor give lessons—though we can set examples—in graceful aging, we can do much to help with issues of financial security, career decisions, training for curricular change, and collegiality between younger and older staff.

Most important, we cannot abandon the seasoned teacher, who offers so much to our schools. Considering that "the graying of the teaching profession" is occurring in independent schools no less than in the public sector (at many schools the average age of the faculty is well into the forties, and one renowned New England boarding school reports an average age of forty-nine), it is all the more important that we focus attention on the needs of our older faculty. When we ask school heads how the seasoned teacher enhances their faculty, they list such qualities as:

- Knowledge of subject matter
- Commitment to an educational career
- Professional attitudes
- Competent classroom management
- More settled lifestyle
- Credibility with parents
- Refined instructional techniques
- Established reputation with students

No longer concerned with "survival," as is the novice teacher, the experienced teacher lends stability and experience, but must also be called upon to give leadership and excellence to our faculties.

What can schools do to help their experienced teachers stay alive and fulfilled? First, school administrators should make it their business to understand adult development in the same way they expect teachers to understand child or adolescent development. Armed with an awareness of the common phases of adult growth, administrators can learn to spot a problem before it becomes a crisis, and to treat teachers in ways that acknowledge and take advantage of their maturation. While seasoned professionals bring a wealth of background and experience to our schools, our responsibility in accepting what they have to offer is to recognize what they need. Part of the job expectation of the division head, dean of faculty, or head of school, depending on the institution's structure, should be to assist people like . . .

. . . Michael, who has been teaching English IV in the same independent school for ten years. He has acquired several titles over the years which have significantly expanded his professional profile, (as well as his paycheck): department chair, curriculum committee chair, director of publications and summer school director. He has been honored and grateful to be entrusted with these important responsibilities. Nevertheless, he has begun to become anxious, worried, and dissatisfied. His myriad responsibilities have made twelve hour days all too common, with no time to explore the literature he loves, to take classes at the university, or to sit in collegial exchange with his peers. Is this how burnout occurs?

. . . Eleanor, dynamic middle school social studies teacher for twenty-eight years. She has always enjoyed a reputation as a superior teacher—creative, energetic, and nurturing. Recently however, she has begun to question her value in the classroom. The fact is, she has begun to feel like an anachronism. The youthfulness of the faculty and administration, the parenting practices of today, the attitudes, and values displayed by students, the changing traditions at school have all contributed to her growing sense of confusion and insecurity. Perhaps she should retire and leave the classroom to the young teachers. Does "old guard" just mean OLD?

Second, schools need to provide new and stimulating work for maturing teachers (not just less work, less coaching, fewer extra-curricular activities, or other such typical adjustments for senior faculty). Among the most exciting opportunities for experienced teachers are the mentoring programs that have proliferated in independent schools in recent years. In addition to providing a better entry into the teaching field for rookies fresh out of college, mentoring programs may give even more to the experienced teacher whose skills are acknowledged and put to new uses, and who is challenged to explain and justify familiar methods to a new and inquiring audience. Curriculum development, service on important committees, especially those involved with planning for faculty development, even such out-of-classroom projects as becoming faculty historian, may validate and rejuvenate an experienced teacher. The essential step in this process has already been mentioned: that the administrator know the teacher involved so as to suggest a project relevant to that teacher's interests and not merely useful to the school.

Professional development outside the school can have similar results. Even a weekend away with experienced colleagues from other schools can enhance an "old pro's" awareness of being part of a profession, and part of a vital cadre within that profession. Many state and regional associations offer Experienced Teacher Workshops or Institutes in a design that was pioneered by David Mallery's NAIS "Experienced Pro" workshops. More extended opportunities, such as the year-long program offered by the Klingenstein Foundation at Columbia's Teachers' College and the year abroad sponsored by the Fulbright-Hays Teacher Exchange, or the summer study grants available from the Council for Basic Education and the National Endowment for the Humanities, as well as the sabbatical programs offered by schools with the financial good fortune to be able to afford them, can turn a career around. (Too often schools assume that it's the dynamic teacher with five to ten years' experience who should be sent off to explore new curricular ideas at a special summer workshop. Try sending the more senior staffer whose knowledge appears rutted in a college curriculum of the fifties or sixties.) Take the classics teacher who was hostile to multicultural curricular efforts until she attended a workshop on blacks in the ancient world and abruptly saw the relevance of the new studies to her own field, or the French teacher whose involvement in a media workshop resulted in his becoming the school's video guru, adding a whole new dimension not only to his language teaching but to that of his whole department.

Most important of all, schools must build a climate in which growth in teaching is expected of all faculty, new and old, and is rewarded by public acknowledgment. Schools which value renewal will permit their faculties to grow from within themselves and from within their schools by providing opportunity and time to contemplate, collaborate, reflect, and grow. As one student of professional development put it, "You can tell a good school from a bad one just by listening to the conversation in the faculty room. In a bad school teachers are made to feel uncomfortable if they try to talk about their teaching; in a good school they're uncomfortable if they're not talking about their teaching.'' Despite a tendency to think otherwise, money is not the determiner of strong programs aimed at professional growth. Many effective programs and ideas from schools across the country can be implemented at little or no cost to the school. Teacher exchanges within schools and with nearby schools, voluntary study groups and reading colloquia, peer observation programs, faculty seminars and presentations, discussion of teaching methods in staff meetings, public praise for teachers who have attended workshops, created new curricula, or experimented with new methods, will keep all teachers, young, and old, developing throughout their careers.

14

Faculty-Centered Faculty Development

by Peggy McIntosh & Emily Style
Co-Directors of the National S.E.E.D.
Project on Inclusive
Curriculum (Seeking Educational Equity and Diversity),
Wellesley College Center for Research on Women

In all the attention being paid to the need for the school curriculum to have more multicultural accuracy, integrity and balance, thoughtful teachers are often made to feel deeply inadequate, aware of all we don't know and were never taught about "others." Yet teachers are not villains. Teachers are part of systems we are asked to change. As educator Deborah Meier of New York City's Central Park East puts it, teachers are expected to continue to drive the school bus while fixing its flat tires.

In the National S.E.E.D. (Seeking Educational Equity & Diversity) Project on Inclusive Curriculum, now in its eighth year, we create seminars for respectful faculty development, over time, planned and coordinated by teachers themselves. If staff development efforts on culture and gender do not take teachers themselves seriously, it is incongruous and unrealistic to think that teachers will, in turn, create more inclusive, respectful environments and curriculum for their students. Faculty-centered faculty development is analogous to student-centered learning.

Emily Style suggested in a 1988 essay entitled "Curriculum as Window & Mirror" that the curriculum can be seen as an architectural structure which schools build around students. Often it provides windows out to the experiences of others but few mirrors of the students' own reality and validity. Given better balance, it can provide both mirrors, which reflect and validate students' various identities and multiple ways of making meaning, and windows out into experiences of "others" and into ways of making meaning and being that are not part of a student's own cultural repertoire. A curricular balance of windows and mirrors helps the young to participate in society with both assertiveness and respectfulness.

It is increasingly clear to us in the National SEED Project that what works for teachers is a staff development process that likewise mirrors teachers' own lives as well as offering windows into new areas that have not, up until now, been part of their schooling or life experience. It is our belief that unless teachers experience themselves at the center of new learning (which draws upon both university scholarship and what Emily Style calls "the textbooks of their lives" as scholarship) they cannot provide curriculum for students which, in turn, puts students' balanced growth and development as cultural beings at the center.

One of us (Emily Style) found that the standard curriculum offered no windows into her mother's life or mirrors for her as a young girl who might be a mother some day. One of the reasons that Style became a teacher was to "do something" with her life, and be unlike her mother who "never worked." Her mother "just" gave birth to and cared for seven children. As a young person in a culture and in school, Style was not in a position to question the silence covering up mothers in the curriculum. She simply received it as a given, oblivious to the damage that it did to her intellectual relation to her mother and to the aspect of herself which would play a caretaking role in culture.

SEED seminar process put Style at the center and took her lifetext seriously. Over time, through reading in women's studies and engaging in monthly conversation with other teachers, Style noticed that school silence had taught her to dismiss her mother intellectually. Eventually, Style interviewed her mother, treating her belatedly the way that school taught her to treat "important people," and subsequently compiling *Mom's History Book* to honor her mother and to balance the record in her own head and for her own daughters.

That document, which makes a textbook of her mother's life, created a respectful window and a validating mirror unlike any other text. The SEED process gave Style permission to take her mother and herself seriously, discovering in the process that (family) life and her own existence were far more complex, multiple, problematic and profound than she had been led to believe.

Fashioning a more inclusive curriculum is inner and outer work, hard work and heart work which makes rigorous demands on memory and intellect. Experienced teachers need respectful professional space to engage with their own life-texts as a fundamental resource. Some teachers have been engaged in just such thinking all along, but in isolation. Most school reform efforts completely ignore teacher and staff (auto)biographies. Becoming part of a community of learners that values autobiographical reflection is a key SEED experience. As Minnesota SEED leader teacher Cathy Nelson explained in a article which appeared in the December 1991/January 1992 issue of *Educational Leadership*:

> [At the SEED Summer Workshop] I became part of a SEED community of 35 learners who teach. Looking at the textbooks of our lives was essential before imagining school climate and curriculums that would more accurately reflect our diverse world. During our first moments together as a community of scholars/learners, we read aloud our personal versions of Caribbean writer Jamaica Kincaid's "Girl," drawing upon the gendered and remembered voices from our own pasts. The first stories we told were our own. The first voices we heard were our own. Immediately we recognized the authenticity and power of our own lived experience.

SEED seminars are led by teachers for their colleagues. They meet monthly throughout a school year for three hours at a time. They offer both window-views out into areas that have not, until now, been part of teachers' formal schooling or their life-texts, and mirrors of their own lives' complexity. They include numerous, brief narratives by participants, told as we go around what becomes "a talking circle." In the conversational nature of this practice, a story told by one participant might become for one listener a window of revelation and for another, a mirror recognition of a once-known landscape, the dim memory of which brightens in the course of the circle conversation.

There are significant dimensions of the personality and the past that are never invited into "professional" conversation in staff development. Due to private reflection, some teachers are aware of the "windows" and "mirrors" of their own learning and teaching process, but most staff development efforts build in no process for either recovering or sharing life-forming knowledge with one's colleagues. SEED seminars are the richer for tapping into this vein of insight and cultural information which is contained within all people and in all school staffs.

At the same time, SEED process offers avenues into the last twenty years of university-based scholarship on gender, race, class, culture and many other diversities of experience. This scholarship illuminates many aspects of cultural power relations. Those of us teaching today are "products" of schooling which embedded in us deep imbalances or obliviousness in regard to matters of cultural positioning and power. The "well-educated" white men on the Senate Judiciary Committee certainly revealed (and some even acknowledged) how inadequately they were schooled to understand what they were hearing in the "hearing" with Clarence Thomas and Anita Hill. Teachers today face an equally daunting task in dealing with all sorts of matters surfacing in schools which our own schooling evaded. Many explosive and political matters assert themselves in today's schools regardless of whether teachers are dealing with a student population primarily composed of "their own kind" or not.

The AAUW report entitled "How Schools Shortchange Girls" (1992) uses the term "evaded curriculum" to label the subjects covered only by powerful silences which, in turn, perpetuate particular positions of gender dominance or mask huge matters of cultural change. In the National SEED Project, we have found that breaking silence about evaded subjects is best done with eminent respect for what is already embedded in the texts of teachers' lives, trusting teachers' ability to talk about these matters as adult learners who are also, in the process, equipping themselves to handle students' life experiences as a central text in schooling. Participating in such a "modeling" experience (in a year-long SEED seminar) enables teachers to do less evading and more educating for real life in their own classrooms than was done for them in their K-12 schooling time.

In a SEED seminar that Emily Style facilitated at Madison High School in New Jersey where she was on the staff for a decade, a European-American teacher revealed that a significant dimension of his identity was being a parent of four children including his thirteen-year-old son who was autistic. Up until then, in his teaching career of over twenty years, no one had ever asked him to speak about his own life-text as the white, male parent of an autistic child. In his own experience of schooling, there had been no windows regarding such a life, nor were there any mirrors in the faculty in-services which he had experienced before the SEED seminar. Isolation and invention characterized his existence.

After this teacher talked from the textbook of his life in the SEED seminar, Style invited him, the following fall, to speak to her American literature classes during their reading of Steinbeck's novel *Of Mice and Men* whose character Lennie could be labeled autistic. This teacher broke more than one silence in Style's classroom in speaking out of the authority of his experience in handling his son's condition and his own experience of parenting. This added (multi-cultural) dimensions to the curriculum that cost nothing in terms of dollars and cents, and benefitted all. In the National SEED Project we have found that the development of teachers as "interior resources" for others in their school buildings (as SEED leader Verdelle Freeman of Piscataway, New Jersey, phrases it) is a critical first step in creating a multicultural curriculum that provides integrity and balance for all staff and all students.

In the SEED Project we try to model respect for teachers' complexities with the hope that teachers will then show the same kinds of respect for their students' complexities. Teachers are not empty vessels any more than students are. Faculty development which ignores a teacher's own complexities and life-contexts repeats the same old errors of the "banking model" (Freire) education which has failed so many students. If we aspire to student-centered learning, we need also to be thinking in terms of faculty-centered learning by teachers. The SEED Project promotes faculty-centered faculty development.

In light of her theory of "Interactive Phases of Personal and Curricular Re-Vision," (1983 and 1990) Peggy McIntosh describes five interactive phases of professional development of teachers which she has come to see through work on gender and culture in the curriculum. They range from the most obliviously authoritative to the most respectful and inclusive. They also constitute a repertoire of ways of working with faculty which have different degrees of appropriateness depending on the task at hand. Phase Theory is adapted here to describe a variety of ways of doing faculty development.

Phase One. Teacherless Faculty Development. "Outside" presenters, "expert" in their subject matter, neither notice teachers nor notice that they haven't.

Phase Two. Exceptional Teachers are featured in faculty development, seen as unusual for their kind (teacher), capable, for example, of "doing multiculturalism" for/in their institution and therefore worth drawing attention to, rewarding and spotlighting. Such exceptional teachers are set apart as Examples (of what most teachers are not).

Phase Three. Teachers as a Problem, Anomaly, Absence or Victim. The administrators let the faculty air their "issues", permitting them to rebel/gripe against school norms and/or "fads" such as multiculturalism. Teachers are expected to attend faculty development events, oblivious of how they are being positioned as problems and/or victims. Faculty development in-service sessions seem to be aimed at "fixing" defective or recalcitrant teachers.

Phase Four. Faculty Lives As Faculty Development. All teachers are seen as having complex lives, encouraged to resort to memory to "make textbooks of their lives" (Style) by narrating their own experiences. Faculty development provides both "windows and mirrors" (Style) for all participants: windows out to the realities of others, and mirrors of one's own reality and validity. Faculty development processes respect memory and a range of emotions in teachers; tap into deep knowledge of inner and outer schooling; enable the recovery of lost worlds. (See McIntosh 1990 Phase Theory paper, for development of her concept of the multicultural interior worlds within each person). Faculty development work filled with intellectual and emotional respect leads to individual healing and institutional vigor. Phase Four is the first phase in which teachers' own stories count as curriculum for faculty development and are not seen "simply" as opinion, complaint, or mere anecdote.

Phase Five. Faculty Development Redefined and Reconstructed to Include All of our Complexities of Self. Phase Five will recognize and use all of our human modes of development, both the vertically-oriented ones identified with "improvement" and the laterally-oriented ones identified with connection and (re)construction of self and society. (McIntosh's Phase Theory essays of 1983 and 1990, and Working Papers # 124 & 219 of the Wellesley College Center for Research on Women, Wellesley, MA.)

With regard to faculty development in multicultural and gender study, Phase One is obviously identified with authority and its functions. In Phase Two, the lines are clearly drawn between the aspiring soloistic self (a possible "winner") and the great undifferentiated mass of "losers." Phase Three, though "issues-oriented" and systemic in its awareness, is not conducive to nurturing deep reflection or the memory of the self-in-construction (McIntosh, 1990); Phase Four recognizes the self-in-relation to others (Jean Baker Miller, 1976), and the self in relation to systems of power, respecting each teacher's response-ability. In Phase Four, the self becomes re-known as a microcosm of a complex world, with the promise of more perceived connection and coherence than at present. As McIntosh has written elsewhere:

> The multicultural worlds are in us as well as around us; the multicultural globe is interior as well as exterior. Early cultural conditioning trained many of us as children to shut off connection with certain groups, voices, abilities, and inclinations, including the inclination to be with many kinds of children. Continents we might have known were closed off or subordinated

within us. The domains of personality that remain can fill the conceptual space like colonizing powers. But a potential for more plural understanding remains in us; the moves toward reflective consciousness come in part from almost-silenced continents within ourselves. (Working Paper #219)

SEED Summer Leaders' Workshops prepare leaders of SEED seminars to travel, emotionally and intellectually, between Phases Two, Three and Four of the consciousness, providing an exhilarating sense of development and reconstitution in teachers. Respectful faculty development is deeply rewarding. Re-construing and re-situating the self as complex transforms thinking and allows for authentic multicultural connections which formal education and society have discouraged in both students and teachers. These interactive processes result in a powerful, grounded impulse toward curriculum re-vision.

Please note that we are not claiming that all cultural differences are contained in any of us, only that we have been, since early childhood, more complex than we have been taken to be, and shaped to be. Since it is impossible to "cover" all types of diversity in the curriculum, it makes sense to start with the inner and outer complexities that the learners in any situation carry within them. For when deep learning, unlearning and relearning occur with one's own life-texts, they yield powerful illumination and educational energy.

Doing intentional multicultural staff development of the caliber we are describing is both a daunting and a nourishing task. As poet Adrienne Rich put it years ago, "No one ever told us we had to study our lives,/ make of our lives a study. . . ." And as she wrote in the same poem, "a lifetime is too narrow/to understand it all, beginning with the huge/rock-shelves that underlie [it] all. . . ."

In the National SEED Project we have found that studying ourselves yields rich multicultural material, lending an exciting contemporary meaning to Socrates' dictum "Know Thyself." In SEED seminar processes, educators respectfully assert, to use McIntosh's phrasing, that "we are all part of what we are trying to change." Such centering is as refreshing and life-enhancing as it is demanding for those committed to multicultural staff and curriculum development.

15

Beyond the Hickory Stick: Discipline in Schools

by Pierre LaTour, Jr., former Assistant Head of School
The Rivers School

"Let the jury consider their verdict," the King said, for about the twentieth time that day.
"No, no!" said the Queen. "Sentence first—verdict afterwards."
"Stuff and nonsense!" said Alice loudly. "The idea of having the sentence first."

Lewis Carroll
Alice's Adventures in Wonderland

I've always liked this scene because it's so perfectly ludicrous. The idea of handing down the verdict before the trial begins stands everything directly on its head and strikes me as being very funny. "Stuff and nonsense" indeed. What's less funny is that, in its own way, justice in Wonderland makes more sense than discipline does in many schools I've known. In the bizarre upside-down world of Wonderland, at least justice is bizarre and upside-down, a peculiar consistency that might be reassuring to the Wonderlandians.

While, the courts reflect the rest of life in Wonderland, too often, discipline in many schools doesn't reflect very much of anything at all. It seems to be one of those things that we need to have but don't like to use, like a toilet bowl plunger, and so we hide it away in a closet and bring it out only in cases of emergency. I don't believe that I've ever heard a tour guide or an admissions officer say to a prospective student or a family, "Now let me tell you about discipline around here."

I'm not surprised. Schools see themselves as warm, supportive, friendly places, and discipline doesn't fit that image. Discipline is what

133

happens when things go wrong; discipline is unpleasant, even painful. Discipline is punishment. But discipline can and should be more than that.

Some years ago, I was part of a committee which had been asked to re-examine the school and to draft a new set of core values and a new mission statement. It was not an easy job, but we finally produced a document that seemed truly to reflect the school's fundamental values and mission. Like every other school, we displayed our mission and our values prominently in the catalog and in the student handbook, and we talked about them in school meetings. But we didn't let it go at that.

Instead of leaving mission and values as remote abstractions, like relics under glass, we used them as the basis for our code of living—our rules—and therefore they became a basis for our code of discipline. Our values and mission not only articulated what we were and what we wanted to be, they also clearly implied what we were not and what we did not want to be. And, when our rules developed directly from our mission and values, discipline, likewise, followed along the same path. Since then, discipline has become, in fact, the clearest outward and visible sign of this school's mission and values. Now, very often in the wake of a serious discipline case, we ask our advisors to meet with their students and to use the case as a springboard for discussion. It must be emphasized that we DON'T encourage a discussion of the details of the case, nor do we ever want to begin a debate on the appropriateness of the punishment. What we focus on are the principles involved: why is the violated rule considered to be so important; which of the school's values does it represent? Some people have complained that these discussions violate the privacy of the individuals involved in the case. What I point out to them is that it's better to place the facts of the case out in the open than it is to let the school wallow in the waves of rumor and exaggeration that usually follow major disciplinary actions. Furthermore, I think that by using cases as a basis for discussion, (we've been doing this for roughly three years) everyone in the school—faculty, students, even parents—has gained a much better understanding of what our values and mission are, and discipline has become more than rules and punishment.

Storming the Battlements: Discipline and the Outside World

It is probably a trick of memory, but I believe there was a time when the outside world—principally parents—had nothing to do with school discipline. The school had its rules, and when one was broken, the school decided on some appropriate disciplinary action. The parents waited for the decision as nervously as the student, and almost always accepted it with a stoicism borne of knowing that there was little they could do about it anyway.

Whether it is the advent of five-figure tuitions or simply a change in the way parents look at schools, things aren't that way any more. Most parents are willing to invest their money in independent education because they believe that it will buy their kids better skills, better college choices and, ultimately, a better life. They see the school as a helpmate, a facilitator, and they become very unhappy when they perceive it as a threat or an obstacle to their child's success.

When their child faces disciplinary action, parents focus almost exclusively on the punishment and its consequences, and almost never on the action that demanded discipline. As a result, the school and the parents usually end up in dialogues where each of them is talking about entirely different things. That rarely leads to understanding.

Some years ago, there was a case involving a senior boy who was caught blatantly cheating on a math exam. Even worse, it was clear that the cheating had been premeditated. After lengthy consideration, the discipline committee stopped short of recommending dismissal and decided instead on a three-week suspension, disciplinary probation and notification of the incident to all the colleges to which the boy had applied. I thought the decision was eminently fair, if not lenient.

I was surprised, therefore, at the father's reaction when I telephoned him with the decision. He began screaming that we "couldn't do this" to his son, that we had "ruined" his son's life, that now no college would ever accept him. Furthermore, he couldn't understand how the school his son loved so much could turn on him and treat him so badly. As a parting shot, he threatened to sue us.

I waited a few hours before calling him back. He was calmer, but when I tried to get him to recognize and to acknowledge the seriousness of what his son had done, all he said was: "He's just a kid, you know," and "I suppose you've never made a mistake."

Even though the boy returned from his suspension, graduated with his class and went on to a successful college career (albeit not at his first choice), the school's relationship with the family was permanently scarred. The boy hasn't visited the school since graduating, and I hear that his father's favorite story at cocktail parties is how the school "screwed" his kid.

In this particular case, I'm not sure that anything could have been done to prevent such an unhappy ending, but it and other cases have taught us some valuable lessons which have served us well since then:

1. *A crisis is not the time to begin discussing values and ethics with a family.* We once assumed that families read the handbook; that they noted, understood and, presumably agreed with the core values and the mission of the school; and that they understood the major rules and how the discipline system operated. That is an assumption we no longer make. Now, each September, we meet with the families of all entering students. We emphasize how important the core values and mission are to us, and point out that their voluntary act of joining us tells us that they, too, accept and understand them. We ask if there are questions (there usually are); we try to keep the atmosphere casual and light, and we follow up with a "nice to see you, thanks for coming" letter. We know very well that all of this is no guarantee against future trouble, but at least no one can say they were never told about the system.

2. *Never discuss a pending disciplinary case with a parent before it has been decided.* It is, of course, important to inform a parent of what has happened; and it's perfectly all right to comfort or to commiserate. What no one should ever do is predict or anticipate the outcome of a case.

I recall a case where a student's advisor, in trying to reassure the parents, told them that because this was the student's first offense, the punishment would probably be minor. What the advisor didn't know was that the case was far more complicated and serious than it appeared. To the parents' surprise, the student ended up receiving a two-week suspension. Surprise turned quickly to rage, and life became far more unpleasant than it ever should have.

3. *Suppress those warm, democratic feelings you've harbored since childhood and keep all disciplinary proceedings behind closed doors.* Not very long ago, we restructured our system of discipline and went from the relative autocracy of a dean of discipline to the republicanism of an elected discipline committee comprised of faculty and students. Falling headlong into the spirit of openness and democracy, we decided it would be perfectly all right for students to have others, including parents, appear on their behalf. We even went so far as to invite parents to attend hearings. We got precisely what we deserved when they accepted our invitation.

At the first hearing, a case involving plagiarism, the accused's mother sobbed throughout the entire proceeding. At the second, a case of vandalism, the accused's father kept jumping to his feet and yelling "Objection!'' each time a member of the committee asked his son a question. There wasn't a third. After the second hearing, the doors of discipline swung shut to all except those directly involved. It was neither an open nor a democratic thing to do, but it has produced peace, and peace is something whose value shouldn't be underestimated.

Fairness and the Doctrine of the Second Chance

By its very nature, a faculty is a debating society with an array of opinions on virtually any issue that concerns the school. Debate on many issues may be challenging, interesting, sometimes hot, but if you want to be sure to unleash passion, simply toss the question of the leniency or the harshness of school discipline onto the floor of the faculty room, then back out quietly, close the door behind you and let the fun begin.

During my nineteen years in independent schools, I think I've seen every weakness or sin a school can commit (except perhaps having a library that's too small) blamed on the severity (or lack thereof) of its disciplinary actions. ''Hard-liners'' greet every decision with a shake of the head and mutter about lack of courage or resolve. So called ''bleeding hearts'' worry about the soul of the school and the rising tide of authoritarianism. Neither group, it seems, is ever completely satisfied.

This is the result, I think, of a fundamental misunderstanding regarding the role of discipline in a school. It is easy to think of school discipline as being analogous to a judiciary system. After all, school discipline is responsible for the enforcement of the laws (school rules) and determines what is to be done when the laws are broken.

Like most easy analogies, however, this one is seriously flawed. The laws of society at large are formulated to protect us from the worst parts of ourselves and to preserve the peace, order and security of the majority when confronted with the depredations of the few. Therefore, punishment is designed with the interests of society at large foremost; the interests of the guilty are secondary.

Independent schools are not accurate reflections of our broader society. While we all have rules which ensure the safety and order of the school community, they are relatively rarely invoked. In my school, for example, the breakdown of serious cases over the past 4 years is as follows:

Off campus without permission	17
Smoking/tobacco use	13
Plagiarism	6
Fighting	4
Cheating	4
Dishonesty	4
Verbal assault	2
Vandalism	2
Disrespect for school policies	1

The overwhelming majority of disciplinary cases involves actions which are essentially "victimless," and discipline, therefore, most often needs to be concerned not with protecting the school community, but with educating the offender, (which often involves educating the rest of the student body as well) and what that requires most of all is flexibility.

Many years ago, during my first term of teaching, the Headmaster took me aside and advised me that the keys to effective discipline were firmness, fairness and consistency. I thought about that for a moment, then asked him if consistency meant that, for the same offense, everyone should be treated in precisely the same way. He smiled and said that yes, that was exactly what he meant. When I asked if that implied that every student in the school was essentially the same, he patted me on the shoulder and said, "In the eyes of the law they are."

That may be so (although I doubt it), but the point is moot. The school isn't the "law," and its students are not a mass of faceless citizens. Most of us have a pretty wide range of kids, certainly in age and, increasingly, in terms of social, religious and cultural backgrounds. To adopt the pose of Justice blindfolded might seem at first to be the fairest way of doing things, but that fairness would be only superficial. In the end, treating every kid the same creates some serious injustices and does a disservice to the concept of school discipline.

Do students deserve a second chance? Sometimes. When they have maliciously and calculatedly harmed someone, when they have purposefully set out to deceive, when they have broken the law, they probably don't. But ultimately it depends on the kid. Most independent schools have the good fortune of being small enough to know their students well. We are there to teach them and to help them grow, and just as we don't try to teach algebra to everyone in exactly the same way, not everyone should be disciplined in exactly the same way either. When discipline focuses on the individual rather than the rule, students may grumble that the system is unfair (how come Joey got only one hour of detention and I got two?), but the grumbling can present an opportunity to point out how nice it is that students are at a place where the individual matters, where things are custom fitted.

Minding our Business: School Rules Beyond the Campus Borders

It is May, a month before graduation. A senior boy is arrested by local police on a Saturday night for possession of cocaine. He claims he is innocent, that the drug was planted on him by someone else. He is released on bail, and his case is scheduled to come to court in August. The story is splashed across all the local papers. On Monday, the boy shows up at school with his father and a lawyer. The headmaster calls me into his office and asks me what we should do. Thankfully, at this point I wake up. It's just another nightmare.

The issue of jurisdiction (and its companion, intervention) beyond campus borders is one of the most difficult we face. Should a school restrict its responsibility for student behavior only to those times when a student is on the campus, or does it have an obligation to hold its students accountable, regardless of time or place, during the length of their enrollment in the school? I think that most of us would agree that the answer is: "It depends." The real question is: "Depends on what?"

I'm not going to answer that, at least not now. Instead, I'm going to present a few scenarios and ask you to decide how you would like to see your school respond to each one. I think that by dealing with specific cases, some general principles may emerge.

Scenario 1 My nightmare, above. Do you allow the boy to remain at school and graduate or do you dismiss him for breaking the school's rule about drugs?

Scenario 2 On Saturday morning, a faculty member sees a senior girl in town smoking a cigarette. She is eighteen, but the school has a specific rule against the "use or possession of tobacco."

Scenario 3 A faculty member comes to you with disturbing news. She has heard several students talking about a huge party this weekend at Billy Jones' house. Apparently, the entire Junior and Senior classes will be there, and there will be all sorts of drugs and alcohol. You know that Billy's parents are in Europe.

Scenario 4 It is early September, just before the beginning of school. One morning you receive in the mail an article clipped from the newspaper of a resort town several hundred miles away. The article is about the trial of a teenaged shoplifter. She is a student at your school. She has been found guilty, but her sentence has been suspended. What do you do?

Each scenario presents difficult choices, and, unfortunately, none of the cases is far-fetched. Situations like these seem to be coming along with ever greater frequency and schools need to be prepared to deal with them. Now that you've decided what you would do, let me describe what I would do and the principles on which those decisions were based. (I emphasize that these are my decisions and not necessarily my school's.)

Scenario 1 I'm going to let the boy return to school and graduate with his class. The principle here is simple and important: a school cannot deprive a student of his or her Constitutional rights. In this case, to act before the court has made a determination of the boy's guilt or innocence would violate the presumption of innocence and deprive him of his right to due process as well. But I would be careful to point out to the student (and to his father, and to his lawyer) that his diploma will be granted based on that presumption of innocence. If he is found guilty at his August trial, the school has every right to rescind the diploma, although an attempt to do so might well lead to some interesting legal challenges.

Scenario 2 I don't like seeing Mary smoking in town, and I probably need to talk to her about the health implications of her habit, but I don't think I can do more than that. The principle here is that a school cannot make rules that supersede the laws of society at large. The school certainly can ban tobacco and smoking on its campus, but it can't tell its students that they cannot do in town what the law says they can. This student is eighteen years old and is legally entitled to smoke.

Scenario 3 I'm going to be the most unpopular person in North America, but I'm going to act. I'll call Billy in and tell him what I've heard. He will, of course, deny it. I will then say that since we're talking about something that isn't going to happen anyway, it shouldn't be difficult for him to call it off. He'll glare at me. Furthermore, I'll say that I'm sure he won't mind if I call his parents in Europe and tell them about things that won't be happening at their house on Saturday night. He'll say, smugly, that his parents are traveling around and can't be reached. I'll say that, in that case, I'm sure that the local police will be pleased to know that Billy's neighborhood will be calm and quiet on Saturday night, and I'll invite them to stop over and see for themselves. Billy will want to strangle me, but I'm acting on the principle that the school is obliged to act in any situation which may threaten the health or safety of its students. If the school knows or strongly suspects that students are going to be engaging in activities which could be dangerous, the school must act. It should notify parents or, if that's impossible, it should inform the local authorities. The kids will hate you for it, and, surprisingly, so will some parents, but legal niceties aside, how would you feel if you did nothing and someone was killed going home from the party?

Scenario 4 This is probably the toughest one of the lot, because I think the school's reaction will depend on how it perceives this student, and I haven't given you enough information about her for that. I do believe, however, that the school has every right to take action, whether that means putting her on some sort of probation or dismissing her from school. One may well argue that this is really none of the school's business because the incident occurred so far away and in the middle of the summer, but I disagree based on the First Principle of Intervention: A school has the right to act when the actions of a student damage the reputation or the well being of the school. Clearly, criminal behavior of any sort is harmful to the school's image, regardless of where or when that behavior may have occurred.

Twenty-five years ago, much of what I've written here would have been regarded as radical or unnecessary. Discipline was punishment for rule-breakers, swiftly and uniformly administered. No ifs or buts and no exceptions. Parents rarely were involved and almost never interfered, and the outside world was far away; we were none of its business and it was none of ours. Discipline has changed because the world of independent schools has changed. We are no longer enclaves of the privileged, walled off from the broader society, and beyond the reach of the outside world. To some extent, we have brought this about ourselves as we have consciously sought to broaden the social, economic, cultural and racial composition of our student bodies. But part of the change has been thrust upon us by a society that sees education as a product (and an expensive one at that) and therefore demands ever greater accountability for every aspect of that product.

We are expected to teach not only the skills that will enable our students to get along in the complex world of the coming century, but also the values and the attitudes that will enable them to lead useful and fulfilling lives. Discipline can and should play a role in that, but only if it goes beyond simple punishment. If it flows directly from the school's mission and core values, if it is a flexible, instructive tool, then it can be comfortably applied even in those cases that make our lawyers wince.

16

Successful Advising: Connecting Fragments

by David C. Black, Head of School
Salem Academy

The words *advising, advisor* and *advisee* will conjure up a broad spectrum of meanings to educators in American schools, ranging from routine activities associated with academic scheduling to complex and demanding processes associated with developmental guidance. Those schools which have taken the time and made the effort to develop comprehensive advising systems have discovered a versatile programmatic tool that can lead to that elusive quality of coherence in a school's overall program. What is advising? What is an advising system? What features do the best systems share? Before answering these questions, let us consider the plight of Marcia, a story of school life with which most high school educators will be familiar.

I was having lunch with my advisees, making heroic efforts to draw out the speechless, attract the attention of a pair who were chatting privately to one another, and generally have a conversation with the whole group. After a couple of false starts, I launched into basketball, since it was tournament time and our school had a good team that year. Marcia, an outstanding sophomore who had already distinguished herself in the classroom and had begun to emerge as a leader in other areas, sat glumly, never raising her eyes from her meatloaf.

Challenged, I waited for the appropriate turn in the conversation to ask her what she thought our team's chances were in the upcoming conference tournament. Everyone turned to hear her response. Nothing. Silence. "Marcia," I ventured. "What?" she grunted. Finally, tears welling up in her eyes, she struggled to ask, "May I be excused?" "Of course," I said, but before I could say anything else, she rushed out.

143

After lunch I had a conversation with the Dean, who agreed that I should arrange to see Marcia that afternoon during her study hall. She came to my classroom at the appointed time, sat in the student conference desk located next to mine, and waited blankly for me to speak.

I began with some reinforcing comments, made a few observations about lunch and her evident distress, and asked if there was anything troubling her that we could talk about. In the next five minutes she unleashed a passionate catalogue of student anxieties and her personal anecdotes related to each: the P.S.A.T., Myers-Brigg ("did nothing but pigeon-hole me"), a mini-term paper and the use of the M.L.A. Style Sheet, quadratic equations, Napoleon's retreat from Moscow, passe compose, Abigail's lines in *The Crucible*, the Spring Fling dance (her so-called friend, Julie, was going with Mark), the suspension of Terry for smoking, and her English teacher's unfair slam of Polonius in *Hamlet*. She nearly hyperventilated on this last one:

> Polonius was *not* a foolish old man—he was a father looking out for his children as well as he could. Horatio was the real fool because he was a wimp, and he was nothing but an enabler for Hamlet's crazy thinking, and I think it's unfair to dismiss Polonius just because it's Hamlet's sick story. Isn't my opinion valid? That's all this is, isn't it? It's not an objective fact. Why is my opinion wrong and his right? I hate this school. . . .

I didn't know what to say.

Unfortunately, overloaded circuitry is not all that uncommon among students in college preparatory schools. Marcia may not be Everystudent, but she shares with a majority of her peers a certain anxiety about the number and complexity of things with which she must come to terms. Schools need to address this fact of contemporary student life because educating means more than filling the vessel—it means bringing the learner to understanding. "Making sense of it all," "seeing the big picture," "understanding the connections between things," "discovering purpose in the disciplines of learning"—and relating it all to the individual's evolving, developing sense of self—this is a tremendous task and one that the best schools work to achieve. One of Marcia's problems, perhaps her biggest, is that she is brimming with information, but it is information that remains compartmentalized and disconnected.

Nearly a decade ago Theodore Sizer pointed to the disconnectedness of school curricula as a principal culprit in the failure of American high schools:

. . . the student sees the curriculum neither as a coherent whole nor as a set of academic imperatives arising from a cluster of subjects. The key question is more often ''What do we have to know for the test?'' than ''What should we know?,'' and what is to be tested is usually factual material: what *is* in Act I, Scenes 2 and 3, of *Lear*. The teacher makes such an assignment because the claims on the sequence of classes he or she has just taught are less those of general qualities of mind than those of immediate specifics. Mastery of these specificities is what leads to a high academic record.[1]

Coherence is not a quality that automatically emerges in an overall school program; it is a quality that must be conceptualized and articulated before it can become a reality. A school's mission statement is often the only place where one can find an articulation of overarching principles, and a mission statement may too easily remain little more than a dusty listing of ideals that gets picked up and polished every five or ten years, or whatever year happens to precede the accrediting agency's visitation. An effective advising system can be a vehicle for achieving the kind of program coherence implied by these principles, and it can also provide the framework of understanding that will help students like Marcia to process the glut of information that bombards them.

Students in a majority of independent secondary schools today, both boarding and day, are assigned to faculty or staff advisors with whom they meet on a more or less regular basis. Although the advisor/advisee relationship has become a common feature of school programs throughout the country, the significance and effectiveness of the advising relationship varies greatly from school to school, and those differing outcomes correlate closely to the varying degrees of conceptualization, goal setting, and administrative leadership found in each school's approach.

In its leanest, least ambitious form, an advising system establishes a formal relationship between a student and a faculty advisor in which it is the advisor's responsibility to meet with the student several times during the school year to distribute grades, review the student's academic performance, and provide a modicum of guidance with regards to the student's future course selections. If an advising structure expects nothing more than this, it will get nothing more. Without clear-cut goals, designed strategies for achieving these goals, staff training, and additional investment of time, the advising function remains perfunctory at best, doing little more than satisfying the need for a pithy paragraph in the school catalogue.

The best advising systems begin with the conscious assumption that advising is an essential part of a school's total program. When advising has become an important and integral part of a school's life, the following elements are always present:

1. administrative leadership and support
2. well-defined goals
3. time investment
4. organizational structure
5. staff training
6. assessment procedures.

Advising remains a function without programmatic substance unless it is provided for by design, and that comes from administrative action. Once advising has been targeted for development, goals and purpose must be defined as a first step. These may differ greatly from school to school, but their articulation provides the conceptual blueprint out of which future action and structure will flow. When purpose has been defined and goals set, a structure of relationships, activities, and time must be formulated. Although the structure of effective advising programs will likewise vary considerably among schools, the investment of time is something that all will share in common. Not only will an effective advising program make time for regularly scheduled advising activities, but it will also make time for staff training and orientation. To be effective, advisors must know what is expected of them, what their purpose is, what goals they should strive to achieve, and what strategies they should employ in pursuing those goals. Finally, schools which ascribe real importance to advising also establish follow-up procedures for assessing the program's effectiveness. Purposeful from start to finish, successful advising programs proceed out of the assumption that there are tremendous benefits to be gained from the structured advising of students.

Before presenting a detailed description of a comprehensive advising program, it would be helpful to define the parameters of the concept of advising as it exists in common practice among independent schools. Although a call to the office of Academic Services at N.A.I.S. will discover very little in the database regarding advising and advising programs, a random telephone sample of schools will reveal that a majority of secondary schools' (and upper school divisions in K-12 schools) advisor/advisee programs proceed from the dual premise that students need academic guidance (course selections, curricular progression, maintaining academic performance), as well as *developmental* or *relational* support.

Thus, an advisor becomes the faculty mentor who helps the student see and understand the expanding contexts of academic life, while developing a relationship with the student that is part booster, part coach, and part sentinel. The common assumption is that the advisor/advisee relationship is a special one in which the advisor performs some school-life "parenting,"—giving advice, explaining, promoting, correcting and making referrals. Dealing with "problems"—conflicts with teachers and other students, overburdened schedules, overlapping commitments and responsibilities—is also a natural part of the advising relationship.

What an advisor is not, however, is a personal or psychological counselor trained to treat or guide therapeutically. Most advising systems draw more or less clear boundaries between advising and counseling, establishing a distinct point in the advising process at which referrals are made to "specialists." If a student persists in a pattern of depressive behavior, for example, an advisor would be expected to refer this problem to another responsible agent, whose job it is to attend to this problem directly or to refer the student to an outside agency or specialist.

Just as advisors are not psychological counselors, they are likewise not learning specialists, trained to diagnose and treat or prescribe corrective and compensatory measures for learning disorders. When an advisor suspects that a student has a special learning problem, then referral is made to a "learning specialist." In some schools this means a specialized L.D. teacher; in others, it means referral to an outside agency or individual. Whatever the case, the advisor's role is to be that of facilitator—the faculty or staff person who knows the student well, is especially aware of the student's strengths, weaknesses, and problems, and acts to direct the student to any special services which he or she may need.

The following detailed description of a comprehensive advising program is culled from numerous models, and it attempts to synthesize the features and practices of the best examples current in independent schools today.

Basic Structure and Time

1. Most teachers and some staff are designated as advisors.
2. Students are assigned to advisors, though some method for choice is usually included.
3. Advisors and advisees have an advisory meeting once a week (30 minutes).
4. Advisors and advisees have a grade conference twice a term (midterm and end of term).

5. Advisors and advisees have lunch together once every two weeks (or dinner in boarding schools).
6. Periodically, advisors take advisees out for a meal or some other entertainment.
7. Advisors meet with advisee parents twice a year.

Advisor's Role/Goals of Advising

1. Advisors serve as school-life mentors for students.
2. Advisors oversee advisees in academic performance, ensuring that the student does not fall through the cracks.
3. Advisors communicate regularly with teachers of their advisees to remain up-to-date concerning advisees' academic status.
4. Advisors communicate with parents—serve as liaison between school and home.
5. Advisors make referrals to administrators or specialists when a problem or need arises that calls for expertise beyond the advisor's capacity.

Advisor Training

1. In-service or workshop orientation (sometimes in the summer, sometimes early in the year) on following topics; A. adolescent development; B. school curriculum and co-curricular program; C. organization and time management; D. study skills; E. behaviors suggesting learning or personal problems in adolescents.
2. Follow-up meetings with person(s) responsible for conduct of the advising program to review topics and discuss.
3. Advisor handbook, more or less summarizing information needed to perform advisor duties.

Special Content

1. Themes such as citizenship, multicultural awareness, liberal arts education, moral courage, conflict resolution, service to others, self-motivation and goal setting, established at the beginning of the year as special topics to be explored in advisee groups. More than one topic may be covered during the course of the year. (The thematic component of an advising program requires training and guidance for advisors).
2. School-wide assemblies scheduled on topics discussed in advisee groups.
3. Advisee group projects on themes explored.

Assessment

1. End of year survey of students
2. End of year survey of advisors
3. Compilation of results and recommendations for subsequent year.

Leadership

1. Commitment from school administration, evident in both time and attention given to the function of advising. One person charged with responsibility to direct and oversee conduct of program (Guidance Counselor, Academic Dean, Division Head, or Head of School).

Miscellaneous Features

1. Advisee bulletin board: to ensure regular (essential) communication from teachers to advisors, a place is set aside in a teachers' lounge or workroom for the exchange of up-to-date information about students. Each advisor is assigned a pouch into which teachers can place notes, forms, etc. about their advisees. A laminated copy of student roll is posted with the name of the advisor next to student's name, making it easy for teachers to pass on information to the right advisors.
2. Budget: advisors are given a budget, usually a dollar amount per student (e.g. $ 15 × 10 = $150.00) from which they can draw to pay for entertainment, etc.

In summary, an effective and comprehensive program of advising like the one just described must have these essential ingredients: 1. leadership (the school administrators must provide the impetus for its development and maintenance); 2. time (adequate time must be set aside for the advising function); 3. staff training (advisors must be given direction, information, and the tools needed to perform the role of advisor); 4. goals (the function of the advisor must be clearly defined in terms of what advising is meant to achieve).

Clearly, the inclusion of thematic content in the advising process adds a dimension to advising that makes it proactive, exploratory, and even instructional. Tapping into the realm of principles, ideals, and overarching values, advising becomes a vehicle for helping the student to understand school life in a larger context, while providing schools with a structured, coherent method of openly addressing the ideals imbedded in the school's mission statement.

Marcia, the anxious and frustrated sophomore described in the beginning, may remain adamant concerning Polonius, overwhelmed by a plethora of facts in her daily life, and charged with indignation concerning life's seeming injustices, whether or not she has the benefits of a program of advising like the one just described. If she *is* fortunate enough to be in a school which strives to take advantage of the educative opportunities afforded by a thoughtfully conceived approach to advising, however, then she may have a much greater chance of successfully holding the disparate elements of her school life together in an integrated whole. Ultimately, advising at its best does just that.

NOTES

1. Theodore R. Sizer, *Horace's Compromise: The Dilemma of the American High School* (Boston: Houghton Mifflin Company, 1984), p. 92–93.

17

Teaching About Human Development

by Carol W. Hotchkiss, Director of Counseling Services
Cate School

Most standard school curriculum deals in some way with human development. Literature tells the story of human experience and archetypal lessons. Science investigates the workings of the human body and our intricate relationships with the physical world. History charts the development of social and political institutions, and the social sciences examine human relationships from a variety of personal, cultural and archeological perspectives. Human development has been expressed through art, poetry, culture, language, music, religion and philosophy. It is through all of these lenses that we teach and learn about what it is to be human.

In the past few decades, several factors have complicated this traditional approach to learning about human development. When we ask parents whether it is easier or more difficult being a teenager today, many assume that while the circumstances have changed, the problems and pressures are about the same. Our students disagree, and, as a counselor and educator working with adolescents in the areas of personal, social and moral development, I have to disagree as well.

Adolescents do face the basic developmental tasks that adolescents have always faced:

1. To form a unique personal and sexual identity.
2. To separate from parents and family.
3. To establish a direction, life/work plan and set of values.

But the societal norms, pressures and possibilities as well as the support systems available to adolescents have changed dramatically over the past

30 years. In many ways, our society itself is going through its own adolescence. There have been some very specific changes in our social realities that have created both positive and negative possibilities for teens today.

- *Birth Control:* The fear of pregnancy is no longer an overriding factor in decisions about sex. A range of birth control methods are legal and available to teens today. That knowledge separates procreation and sexuality whether or not teens have the forethought, self-assurance, comfort level, income or maturity to actually use the birth control that is available. The statistic that four out of ten girls will get pregnant while still in their teens suggests that this is a very significant difference.
- *Abortion:* Even when birth control fails or is not used, legalized abortion further removes teenagers from the reality of creating and taking responsibility for a baby. Statistically, one out of every five girls in the U.S. today will have an abortion before she is 20 years old.
- *AIDS:* Most teenagers today had little sense of sexuality before they knew about AIDS. Through our fear and the political realities of AIDS, many third- and fourth-graders learn about sex through admonition and complicated concepts of sexual preference, protective devices and graphic descriptions of various safer or not safer sexual practices. This is probably both frightening and confusing, and many students today enter teenage sexuality with a look of war-torn cynicism and impotence.
- *Sexuality in Our Society:* Teenagers have not created their preoccupation with sex. They have grown up with it in almost every area of their lives. The average media viewer sees 9,000 scenes of suggested intercourse per year. Music, movies and TV are explicitly sexual. Sex is used to sell even the most non-sexual items and often teenage or child models are used as sexual enticements.
- *Children of Divorce:* Almost 50% of the students going through schools today have experienced at least one parental divorce. Aside from the temporary disruption of family life, this process seems to have had a more subtle impact on many of these students. They tend to be cynical and slow to trust the adults and institutions around them. Many fear intimacy and have a strong need to be independent.
- *Single Parents:* With divorce, many parents begin to date and have new sexual relationships that may be initially awkward in a traditional home setting. Distinctions between adult and adolescent be-

havior may become blurred, and many parents share the confusion and diffusion of modern sexual values. Parents become openly sexual people, and our students can no longer deny this reality.

· *Acceptability of Drugs and Alcohol:* Along with sex, our standards and expectations about drugs have significantly relaxed since the 60s. Children begin to experiment with alcohol and marijuana in sixth and seventh grade and close to 90% have tried marijuana before they graduate from high school.

· *Availability of Drugs and Alcohol:* Just about any student in any school in the U.S. today can get hold of most illegal drugs if she or he wants to. For the majority, it is not difficult and for many, the opportunity will present itself with little or no effort of their own. Friends supply friends, and there are always adult sources around to help out. Most teenage parties, like their adult counterparts, include some availability of alcohol or drugs.

· *Changing Sex Roles:* There are many new and enriching opportunities for both men and women as we question and rethink our traditional gender roles, but this creates fewer traditions or clear expectations for young people attempting to form an initial sense of adult gender identity. This ultimate freedom to form and be themselves can feel somewhat overwhelming and contradictory at times.

· *An Affluent Economy and Delayed Adulthood:* Even in times of economic concern, the U.S. is a country of relative privilege and affluence. Our students *have* more and *earn* less than any previous generation. Accustomed to being given most of what they need and much of what they want, it is often difficult for young people to establish a sense of worth and values.

· *Social Awareness:* At the same time, students today have grown up with a sense of overwhelming problems and vulnerability, from global warming and ecological concerns to the unending presence of foreign wars and nuclear power. Many teenagers consciously or unconsciously, do not believe that they will actually live to full adulthood. This can leave them with a sense of helplessness and immediacy, preoccupied with pleasure, immediate gratification and personal advancement.

· *Ethical Standards:* The cry for "family values" comes from a widespread lack of values throughout public institutions. Personal scandals don't surprise anyone and are broadcast to sell newspapers, TV talk shows and the nightly news. Our students have been raised in an era of socially accepted amorality. Just about anything is OK as long as you don't get caught.

Some of these changes are clearly negative and regrettable while others may seem like a price that we pay for basically desirable advances. In either case, these circumstances create the fabric of our society that our students must live with and learn from. At the same time, there have been changes in the traditional support systems that socialize young people and help them develop as new members of this transitional society.

- *The Family:* The family has always been the primary institution of socialization and support. While there have always been "dysfunctional" families and there have always been some children without a family at all, the nuclear family has been under special pressures during the last thirty years. The adjustments to divorce, remarriage, and step families tax a child's trust and reliance on family adults. The geographic mobility of families today also separates extended family members or one parent may live far away. Very often, children, and parents trying to raise children, do not have a network of grandparents, aunts, uncles and cousins to turn to. With two working parents or a working single parent, there is a lack of regular supervision and casual availability for many of our students. Busy schedules, work and activities reduce the likelihood that a family will sit down together for a family meal even once a day. And, for a variety of social and economic reasons, the American family is programmed to self-destruct. There is a general focus on independence and separation, not connection and resolution.
- *Religion:* Religion has also been a traditional transmitter of social values and traditions, but many of our students and their families have chosen not to be involved in religious training or social groups. Religion and spirituality or ethics are not necessarily equivalent, but one of the consequences of this shift from religious training has been that many students get little or no formal training in values or the spiritual nature of human life. There is no regular time set aside to formulate individual or group values or to pause and reflect in the day-to-day rush of human activity.
- *Community:* Most communities no longer provide the sense of being known and held accountable for adolescents growing up today. Urban and suburban life creates barriers of economics, diversity and sheer numbers. There are just too many people to know and be known. Even elementary schools often have over a thousand children. With-

out this connection and accountability, students do not establish mentors in neighbors, store clerks, club leaders or older community heroes around them. They are not validated, scolded, esteemed and advised by a community of adults who are concerned and involved with their upbringing.

• *Social Standards and Role Models:* Every social group has its norms and unspoken rules of conduct and values. Without the underlying institutions of family, religion, and community, our culture has proven too diverse and disconnected to establish any consistent standards. Our political, athletic and religious leaders are often involved in amoral or immoral behavior. There is no common ground of ethical behavior. As students grow up today, adult standards are inconsistent, and there are few universal guidelines or sacred traditions or values to lead the way.

Schools are the most consistent, adult-connected influence in the socialization of young people today. The problems and pressures that young people bring to our schools often disrupt and undermine traditional educational approaches. We can't teach kids when they are stoned or depressed or afraid to take risks. Amoral individuals don't know how to work honestly and cooperatively in our school communities. Sexual and chemical pressures distract our students from developing their intellectual capabilities. Low or achievement-dependent self-esteem further reduces an individual's ability to integrate and control all of these pressures.

Many schools are responding to these circumstances by incorporating courses on personal responsibility, sex and drug education, individual wellness, ethics and values into their standard curriculum. Over the past ten years, Cate School in California has developed a four-year curriculum that attempts to address each of these concerns in developmentally appropriate times and ways. The needs, questions, cognitive ability and experiential readiness of students change dramatically over the four years of high school, so we have attempted to focus on different information, issues and values in each of the four grade levels. Our primary goal for each of these programs is to provide a forum for honest discussion of developmental issues, the dissemination of accurate information and the opportunity to explore these issues within a realistic social and ethical context. The Freshman and Sophomore Seminars and the Junior Retreat are all required of all of our students and the Senior Teaching Assistants are selected from a pool of interested applicants.

This developmental curriculum has evolved piece by piece over the last ten years and continues to change to meet the needs and questions identified by both students and faculty. The curriculum started out as a single course in the sophomore year to address the human biology of wellness, sexuality and drug use. The first class to complete this course suggested a follow-up retreat the following year to look at issues of drug use, social factors and responsibility in a more personal way—the first Junior Retreat. This class also politely pointed out that students did not suddenly discover these questions and concerns in their sophomore year—freshmen and women needed to have a forum to explore the rather pressing concerns of their growing independence, pressures and responsibilities. By the third year, we had a Freshman and Sophomore Seminar and a three-day Junior Retreat in place. With growing support from the faculty and a strong interest among the students, we were able to recruit a number of seniors to train to be our teaching assistants in the two underclass seminars. The next seven years were filled with trial and error and an increased understanding of the process of educating students to make healthy, responsible choices about their well-being, relationships and values.

At this point, our Human Development curriculum includes:

FRESHMAN SEMINAR: This class meets twice a week for a full year in sections of eight to twelve students with a male and female Senior Teaching Assistant and one full-time teacher. It is required, but non-graded with no homework obligations. Students view the course as a time to wind down and share their current concerns, obstacles, trials and successes. The course helps to establish the norms of open communication, honesty and cooperation. Topics covered include:

Adjustment And Mastery In A New School
Study Skills And Self Discipline
Self-Esteem And Personal Responsibility
Support, Cooperation And Respect In Relationships
Personal And Group Values And Standards
Personal Identity And Goal Setting.

SOPHOMORE SEMINAR: This class meets twice a week for a full year in sections of eight to twelve students with a male and female Senior Teaching Assistant and two part-time teachers—one whose specialty is human biology, the other trained in social and psychological issues. It is a required and graded half-credit course with homework expectations. Students write a weekly opinion paper expressing their views, have short reading assignments and take four unit tests to be sure they have mastered the information presented. This course provides biological and psychological information on individual wellness, sexuality and drugs as well as equal opportunity to talk openly with each other about these issues. While information is critical to responsible decision-making, students relish the opportunity to honestly share their thoughts, feelings, questions, experiences and dilemmas. Topics covered include:

Personal Wellness And Responsibility
Nutrition And Diet
Exercise And Fitness
Biological And Cerebral Physiology
Drug Use And Abuse
Codependency And Enabling
Sexuality And Relationships.

JUNIOR RETREAT: This is a three day retreat in the late fall attended by all Juniors and 15–18 faculty volunteers that addresses issues of chemical dependency, personal relationships and communication and leadership. Students and faculty meet in small groups and as a full group to explore each of these issues. We have a panel from Alcoholics Anonymous, some of which are Cate graduates, and run a full group Alateen meeting during one of the evening sessions. The Head of School often holds a "town meeting" discussion of a related issue of current concern and we usually lead the groups in provocative simulation exercises on power, leadership and privilege. There is time to play and talk and reflect on the values and experiences evoked by these sessions. This is a powerful and enjoyable weekend which inevitably establishes new bonds of communication and trust within the class and with the faculty. The Junior Class organizes a fund-raising effort to raise over $2,000 towards the cost of this weekend—an activity which provides a concrete opportunity for cooperation and leadership.

SENIOR TEACHING ASSISTANTS SEMINAR: The Senior T.A. program is an elective offered by selection in grade twelve to students who are willing to be concerned and informed resources for underclassmen. Selected seniors are assigned in male/female pairs to either a Freshman or Sophomore Seminar section—we have eleven sections, so we can accept 22 seniors, a difficult and thoughtful process as we usually have more than twice the number apply. While the program is certainly open to students who are traditionally selected for leadership positions, it also provides an active leadership opportunity for those whose more non-traditional strengths with their peers might not otherwise be utilized. It is a full year, credit course that meets twice a week with the seminar classes and twice a week for training and class preparation. T.A.s assist with seminar activities, teach part and full lessons and serve as resources and peer counselors to the students in their section. This is a very popular program which tends to foster a genuine sense of responsibility and concern for younger students. Training for the T.A.s includes sessions on:

Peer Counseling Skills
Information On Local Resources And Organizations
Learning Disabilities And Academic Skills
Sexual Harassment And Assault
AIDS And Other STDs
Alcohol And Other Drugs
Eating Disorders And Body Image
Relaxation And Managing Stress
Racism And Issues Of Diversity
Gender Issues
Grieving And Loss
Depression And Suicide
Divorce And Family Issues
Ethics, Power And Privilege.

As a result of this curriculum, I have compiled a workbook—*Quests and Quandaries*—which contains information, exercises and values-related questions which we found useful and relevant. This text is not intended to define a specific curriculum, but contains interrelated topics that can easily be taken in whatever order a particular program requires. We jump around, using different sections in different contexts—some in class or small groups; others can be done individually or for training purposes. Readings may be assigned to precede, follow or supplement a lesson. There is a companion *Curriculum Guide* which we use to help train our T.A.s and prepare for our lessons and activities. It includes sample lesson plans, supplementary activities, resources and suggestions for evaluating what students have learned.

These texts evolved out of our own need to consolidate the topics, activities and process that we use in our curriculum into one source—integrating personal development, biology, reflection and values. But I intentionally organized them so that the material can easily be adapted and used as a base for a variety of programs that address these issues.

Every school population, philosophy and curriculum is unique. Any program or materials must be tailored to your specific set of needs and objectives. *Quests and Quandaries,* as well as the human development curriculum that I have described above, are presented as a springboard and set of tricks and experiences to help you develop the curriculum that will address your own specific resources, goals and needs.

Students need our direct and honest attention to these issues. They need to learn the skills and value of healthy relationships and responsibility for their physical, emotional and ethical well-being. They need to respect and listen to each other, to learn to speak honestly about the concerns that are important to their lives. As adults and as schools, we must provide the leadership and opportunity for our students to actively explore these issues. There are many ways to do this and the process is fascinating and rewarding. Visitors to our seminars are always impressed with the openness, respect and intelligence of our lively student discussions. The curriculum values of communication, cooperation, reflection and personal integrity inevitably filter into other aspects of our school community—other classes, dormitory life, student government and social interactions. Seniors become protective, concerned and involved with our younger students. Classes share a real bond of trust and shared dialogue.

There are many important questions and obstacles in establishing an effective Human Development Curriculum. Strong administrative support is very important and a committed core of faculty who is willing to work and persevere on this aspect of a student's education is essential. Listen to your students and enlist their support and investment. Look at your time restrictions and figure out ways to make this curriculum a legitimate part of your school day and workload—otherwise, it will get lost. We have found parents to be a very supportive and helpful part of our program. Develop interactive activities that strengthen their understanding of your school program and communication with their children. Our Parent's Day classes always actively involve parents in the type of discussion and activity that we use in our classes, and we occasionally give "homework assignments" for students to interview and discuss important issues with their parents. If you can possibly arrange it, use seniors to help you teach, develop and evaluate your program. Their insight, commitment and relationships with the students in your classes are absolutely invaluable.

Most importantly, do something. Make mistakes and learn from them. Get faculty talking and arguing about the process, possibilities and responsibilities of educating whole, healthy, responsible and ethical young men and women. Don't expect everyone to instantly rally around this new agenda—there are always pragmatic and political objections, and some people will never believe that schools are an appropriate forum for "non-academic" issues. Build slowly with manageable objectives, and constantly evaluate what works and what doesn't. Identify your strengths and resources. Be realistic about your hurdles and limitations. Talk to teachers involved in programs at other schools; take bits and pieces of ideas that interest and appeal to you. Commit yourself to learning, listening and making something happen. Let your students know that their physical and personal health, the quality of their relationships and the integrity of their values are an essential part of their education.

Quests and Quandaries: A Human Development Workbook and its companion *Curriculum Guide* are published by Avocus and can be ordered by calling 800–345–6665.

18

Student Leadership

by Edward R. Costello, Head of School
University School of Nashville

One cannot escape the term *leadership* in our schools. In our mission statements, we often claim it is part of our purpose to train leaders. We may promise or imply we will somehow instill it in our students. Many of our parents are seen and see themselves as community leaders. In educating their children, our schools accept the burden of preparing a new generation of leaders. At least some of our students expect to be able to exercise leadership within the school. They may even be asked to write about it on a college essay. And yet it is an illusive quality students probably define differently than do teachers or administrators. Very often, adults think a student exhibits leadership ability when he or she somehow convinces other students to follow institutional expectations. Whereas in the world of the student, finding creative ways to avoid those expectations might easily mark a student as a leader. Students who don't pass adult leadership tests may easily come under criticism and feel inadequate. I remember a team captain, after a particularly devastating loss, complained that the problem was "no one treats me like a leader." I was tempted to say "That's because you're not," but thankfully held my tongue. He was miscast in his captain role, and, of course, I had a big part in placing him in it.

I have a vivid memory of one test of leadership posed to us by our principal during my own years in high school. In the spring of one year, some boy or boys had gotten in the habit of knocking the hand-towel dispenser off the bathroom wall. After several unsuccessful attempts to affix the dispenser to the wall in such a way as to prevent its being knocked off, our principal called an assembly of all the boys in the school. This was the first and only such gathering any of us had ever taken part in, and we were sufficiently chastened as we entered the auditorium, knowing only that the gathering itself was an ominous sign. We were clearly not headed to an all-male awards assembly. After giving us the details, our principal said: "This behavior really burns my cork"; and he posed a challenge for us to exert some leadership in the form of self-policing. He decided to hang the dispenser on the wall by one strand of wire. Anyone could simply lift it off should he choose. It was up to those of us who were on the side of law and order, and dry hands, to keep it on the wall, because he was never going to have it refilled or put back otherwise.

His experiment lasted about ten minutes. There was a race to the bathroom, between those who had been busy knocking the thing down and those who had just figured out a great way to burn the principal's cork, to see who could get their hands on the towel dispenser first. Although some of us probably would have enjoyed being able to dry our hands, no one was foolish enough to exercise the sort of leadership our principal was calling for.

Twenty years later, I found myself standing in the middle of 360 high school students making a similar plea. I don't even remember the issues, but I think it was admonishing students not to park their cars in spaces marked for visitors, complete with the philosophy of why we needed to welcome all guests for the greater glory of the institution. Some students may have avoided using those spaces, but I'm confident others filed the information away under anti-institution behavior to exhibit and perhaps flaunt when the occasion presented itself.

Students who behave this way are likely to be acting appropriately, in a developmental sense, since they need to be testing institutional limits and questioning standards set by adults. Many of them also have excellent organizational and leadership skills, although they may be very reluctant to use them in the formal ways we generally provide for them.

Students do not always accept the same measures of leadership that faculty members often use. Early in my career, I attended an evening faculty meeting devoted to naming the winner of the school's major award for leadership, an award which was a large trophy. Several different students were put forth as appropriate recipients, and their respective merits were weighed at great length and with marked animation by those who had nominated them. As we were leaving the meeting, we met some students on the campus who asked us what we had been doing, and we explained. One kid remarked simply, "Oh, yeah, you people can never decide who should get the Suck Cup."

The fact is that our schools are full of kids who have the potential to exercise leadership and who will be leaders in their adult lives. There are not enough conventional and formal leadership positions in our schools to go around. It is not surprising that many very influential student leaders prefer to exercise their gifts in informal ways rather than to seek appointment, anointment, or election to positions endorsed by the adults in the community. As the student chairperson of the prom committee seeks to gain support to rent a downtown hotel for the event, there is usually a student, chairing what is called the ''non-prom committee,'' who is seeking to convince seniors not to attend at all.

Elected student leaders, team captains, student publication editors, and club presidents are certainly exercising leadership capabilities as they manage their duties of marshalling students' abilities to accomplish a wide variety of useful goals. These sorts of responsibilities can and should be maximized. For example, at University School of Nashville, we have a school-wide election for student council officers and representatives. Although not everyone who runs is elected to the council, full membership is open to anyone who attends four consecutive meetings of the group. A student may thus become a member by voting with his or her feet. Participation becomes a sorting device rather than an electoral process in which some students would routinely choose not to take part and the group can escape the danger of exclusivity.

Indian Springs School in Birmingham, Alabama has adopted the commission form of student government. This choice was made on the grounds that a school is a kind of small town, to which the commission system is uniquely suited. The school has a mayor, who is the chief executive officer in charge of coordinating the work of the various commissions. Commissions cover the important areas of school life—education, service, citizenship, protection, recreation—and include a student judiciary. Mayors are rarely elected without first having served successfully as commissioners, experience which has given them the chance to exercise leadership in a public way and also allowed them to establish a record on which to base a candidacy.

Two important features of this system are worth noting. The commissioners are charged with monitoring important aspects of school life. If the commission charged with running the prom doesn't function, then there is no prom. Students may learn as much from failing in a task as from having adults come to the rescue. The commissioners and mayor also stand for reelection in the middle of the school year. This practice allows more students to serve in visible leadership roles as well as to face the judgment of their peers based upon their performance in office.

Several day schools, including Greenhill in Dallas and Isadore Newman in New Orleans, have found an additional arena for student leadership in their peer helper programs. Students may be required to apply for and interview for positions as peer leaders, but the training can also be offered within the curriculum as a course. Students study group interactions and explore their own feelings regarding content-based lessons on current social issues, such as death and dying. This training is extensive, and requires a major time commitment from the students. Upon completion, peer helpers, normally juniors, then lead groups of younger students in discussions ranging from life at the school to life in general. The younger students may be required to attend these groups, which may or may not have adult observers. The program recognizes that younger students are powerfully influenced by the opinions of older students and that no subject is out of bounds, as they interact both inside and outside the school walls. Getting the older students to consider and challenge thoughtfully their own opinions and biases before they freely make them available to their schoolmates makes a great deal of sense. Putting them in charge of groups which meet on school time also helps them to recognize both the power they have and the responsibility they have to exercise it wisely.

The groups are theirs to run in large part as they see fit, and the conversations are confidential. The leaders are debriefed by the counseling staff, as often as weekly, to discuss specific issues within the groups and to provide positive results for both the younger and older students involved.

The University School of Nashville sponsors a leadership retreat each year, a two-and-one-half day event which begins the second Thursday in September and ends on the following Saturday. All high school students are invited, and about 25 percent normally attend. Speakers are invited to discuss concepts of leadership and the students participate in activities and share concerns about their school and community. From this experience, students are encouraged to pursue themes and issues for the school year which will be addressed in assemblies or community meetings. It is even possible that an academic day be devoted to a topic of significant interest. For example, as a result of the retreat two years ago, the students sponsored a day-long program devoted to issues of human sexuality, including AIDS, sexually transmitted diseases, date rape, and gay and lesbian lifestyles. Students were responsible for finding and inviting appropriate individuals to present the various topics. The day was a huge success, because it was born from student interest and carried our by invested students who saw the value in creating a program of high quality.

Central to any plan which has students exercising leadership in the creation of meaningful programs is the idea that time must be reserved for some discovery process to occur. Retreats take students from classes. Required peer helper meetings may shorten lunch periods or impact when clubs and others activities can meet. The point is that those things valued by the school will be given time to flourish. Those deemed less important will be forced to compete for time, perhaps by being attached to the end of the school day.

Another key element in giving students the opportunity to exercise leadership is to allow them to tackle issues and problems which have a tangible impact upon the life of the school. Failure will be more significant perhaps, but success will also be more real. This lesson was learned in the boarding school several decades ago, when the self-help system was invented to put students in charge of the daily care and routine maintenance of the physical plant. If the dishes were not washed after dinner, no one had clean plates for breakfast. Leadership does not exist in a vacuum without a purpose. The more necessary the task, the more real the experience of leadership in its accomplishment.

19

The Crazy Years: What Works in Middle Schools

by Ruth Huyler Glass, Upper School Head
The Langley School

It's 7:15 on a Wednesday morning in February. Circled around a large table are six teachers, one administrator, two parents, and a somewhat apprehensive student. Despite his nervousness, this young man is not "in trouble." His grades have slipped noticeably, however, and recent communication between school and home has suggested that there is some discrepancy between the story that he tells at home and that which he brings to school. It's time for a "summit conference." This one has been requested by the school, but the boy's parents easily could have initiated the gathering. The next hour will be spent developing a plan to reorient the student, including specific responsibilities on the part of each person in the room. The conference will be followed by a letter written to the parents detailing expectations on both sides, and the faculty will receive a copy of summary notes.

The fact is that the scenario described might reflect a child with serious problems were we talking about either lower or upper school. In middle school the pattern is a familiar one, however, reflective only of a child struggling with hormones and an appropriate desire to gain some independence from the parents whose advice he actively sought just two years earlier. Very few of us would like to relive our own middle school years. Effective independent schools provide the best system of support possible for both parents and students at this puzzling stage of life, run by experienced experts who demonstrably prefer working on this level.

When I tell people that I am a middle school teacher and administrator, the inevitable response is, "You must be crazy!" Perhaps, although I am more inclined to consider my colleagues and myself as involved in the most challenging, exciting stage of education. The reaction is typical of the general misperception of middle school students and, therefore, that division in any school. Fortunately, there is a national movement which has begun to address both the needs and strengths of this level in a way that finally respects its differences at the same time it challenges schools to accommodate them. Not surprisingly, many independent schools are way ahead of the public schools in their own revolutions for middle school education, but for many the changes have been minor and representative of token adjustments, not an appreciation for this distinct and formidable stage in life. In order to be effective, schools must establish carefully prescribed programs which incorporate several proven elements of success: good faculty; a schedule and curriculum reflective of adolescent needs, interests, and learning styles; an advisory system; faculty meetings which are scheduled and structured with the students as a priority; good record-keeping; open communication between home and school; parent education; specific goals for making the transition to high school; and professional development opportunities for staff.

Middle School Faculty

Teachers and administrators who work with middle school children effectively should be hired using some significantly different criteria from those required on lower and upper school levels. The patience and "mothering" essential for younger children must be replaced by an unusual degree of flexibility, nurturing that provides a home base without an encircling arm, an unfailing sense of humor, and seemingly limitless energy. They need thick skins and the recognition that much of the time they will be considered "in the way" by their charges. They must be willing to be "the bad guy" as a matter of course, as their charges constantly test limits.

The mastery of subject that contributes to outstanding teaching on the upper level is less important for middle school teachers than it is for them to be well-educated in general, have an enthusiasm for their subject, and be willing and able to teach to a variety of learning styles. When I am hiring for the middle school, I look for teachers whose clear first choice is to teach on that level. With a few notable exceptions, transplanted upper school teachers will constantly battle what they consider to be a lack of seriousness and respect for their subject.

A wonderful story told by a middle school principal in a fine independent school illustrates the nature of the beast and the requirements of a good teacher. He tells of a young male art teacher in his all-girls school who presented his 7th grade class with an arrangement of fruit as a subject for a still life drawing. He left the room for a few moments and returned to discover the girls had eaten the fruit. He resigned that same day. He should have (first) not left the room or (second) celebrated the class's creativity and cheerfully held them accountable by having them draw the peels, seeds, and cores. Teachers or administrators who don't see the humor in that story belong on a different level.

Beginning the Day

Most middle schools have switched from a homeroom environment to departmentalization. Schools which include 5th and 6th grades in their middle division might consider a modification of that system, and in all grades on this level it is essential to provide a consistent base of operations for all students. Whether students gather in homeroom or advisor environments during their day, they need to touch base with a single teacher and a constant group of peers.

At Langley the first fifteen minutes of the day are spent in homerooms, where announcements are read, books and homework organized, attendance taken, business discussed. Middle school children are notoriously disorganized, forever leaving books and papers strewn around campus. The students who have the most difficulty making it through the day are those who arrive late and spend the morning trying to settle themselves. An additional benefit of this system is that teachers are provided the opportunity to observe any children who might be particularly off kilter, as well as to discover which ones leave homework until the last minute. It helps to have a similar departure system, though that, realistically, is much more difficult, given sports and other activities.

The Curriculum

Recent studies and long experience both indicate that the curriculum on the middle school level *must* be adapted to the interests and attention spans of its students, and effective middle schools have developed programs which vary significantly from those in the upper school, even while they are departmentalized. Curricular innovations which are the most positive can be scheduling nightmares, but if the needs of the students are truly to be met, they must be a priority.

Middle School students learn best in environments which are experiential, in which they are required to think and perform and their opinions are respected, and in which they have blocks of time to work in groups. Maintaining consistent classes provides a basis for team and group work throughout the curriculum.

At Langley, science and math classes meet four days a week but for five periods, providing a double lab period in each. Students in science spend time designing and conducting legitimate experiments or taking field trips such as a recent 7th grade excursion to a local hospital to observe open heart surgery performed by one of the parents. Simulation games, debates, and student-produced videos representative of various time periods form the core of social studies class time.

The less studied in isolation, either from a student or teacher perspective, the better. As an example, our 8th graders recently completed a unit on The Civil War, with an emphasis on the Battle of Gettysburg. For English they read *The Killer Angels*, by Michael Shaara; in social studies they re-enacted the debates leading to the secession of the South; they took a trip to Gettysburg where they made sketches for art which they later turned into woodcuts. Next year we will add a science component to the unit in which students will study the effects of the environment and topography on that battle.

Teachers who prefer to work in isolation or whose method of delivery revolves around lecture and note-taking will not be effective in the middle school. Any subject and its accompanying facts, figures, and concepts is the vehicle for developing critical attitudes toward learning and habits of study which will carry students into the upper school. The challenge to administrators in good independent schools is to establish and articulate a philosophy of education specific to the middle school which is supported by faculty and yet which is open and responsive to the ever-growing and changing developments in middle school awareness.

Advisories

Long an established part of good upper schools, the notion of advisories in middle schools has met with some surprising resistance. To be truly effective, a middle school *must* incorporate these systems in their program. The structure of advisories varies as widely as the number of schools which incorporate them. What is essential for success is that individual schools establish with their faculties what is appropriate for them, and that they remain committed to the philosophy.

At Langley, groups are co-ed and comprised of 6th-8th graders. Unless there is a specific request otherwise, students keep the same advisor for their entire career in that division. We meet together at least twice a week as a group. Advisors establish academic goals with advisees, discuss topics ranging from formal presentations related to alcohol and drug awareness to whatever is on kids' minds, and take their groups three times a year to a soup kitchen in Washington, D.C. (leaving campus at 6:15 A.M.). Most important, they serve as students' advocates and are expected to be a part of any disciplinary actions or communications snafus with other teachers.

In many schools, students select their advisors each year. Some co-ed schools elect to have single-sex advisor groups. I repeat: the format doesn't matter if it is one in which the school believes. At this stage, however, middle schools without strong advisor programs are questionable. Students need clearly defined means to connect directly with individual adults upon whom they can depend.

Faculty Meetings

Individual students should be discussed at regular intervals during faculty meetings. Not only students of concern, but also those for whom it is believed all is going well should be mentioned. Often the biggest clues to impending problems can be recognized through a simple observation that is then seconded or expanded by another adult. A minor out-of-character incident may be just that, unless, for example, it suddenly appears that a student is not handing in homework across the board.

At our school, we in the middle school meet with the fifth grade teachers at the end-of-year faculty meetings so that they can share their accumulated knowledge about personalities, study habits, and parental expectations. It has also been my experience that in good schools, spending time sharing concerns about a student in trouble bonds a faculty. While interpretations and prescriptions may vary, faculty in healthy schools demonstrate a shared mission and philosophy even as they explore distinct frustrations. Administrators should pay heed to significant schisms among teachers as they discuss children; too much may signal a support system that is, itself, suffering.

At our school, the administration and athletic department have compromised to ensure that all coaches—classroom teachers, themselves—can attend faculty meetings. Divisional faculty meetings are now held every two weeks on Monday afternoons following school, and the athletic department does not schedule games for those days. The input of coaches is invaluable to understanding the complexities of young adolescents. Some schools require all classroom teachers to coach a sport or be similarly engaged in drama or music activities, enabling students and faculty to gain a much better appreciation of each others's talents and interests.

Records

Good schools maintain excellent records that are readily available for faculty. Much as one expects a doctor to be able to treat a patient more effectively and quickly if she has a medical history at hand, so one can expect a teacher or administrator to address both strengths and needs of a student if there is an accurate record of them. Files should include transcripts, summaries of parent conferences, medical histories, testing, and anecdotal material that might relate to social and/or emotional development. A student making his or her way through a school should be followed by an ongoing paper trail.

In our school, advisors are asked to maintain the student files. At the opening faculty meetings in September, they are required to summarize any special needs a child might have—specifically as a result of diagnostic testing. Administrations must stress with faculty the need to keep anecdotal observations. It's amazing how quickly yesterday's disruptions meld with today's and tomorrow's.

Communication

Effective communication requires commitment to a philosophy that home and school are working together to ensure the best education for each child, and that cooperation in this effort is essential. Perhaps this is the area that most reflects the notion of "educating the whole child." Good news as well as concerns should be communicated regularly, whether it be by phone or in writing. As an administrator, it can be disheartening to call a parent only to have her acknowledge my presence with a fearful,

"What's wrong?" When I am doing my job well, I make a point of contacting parents whose children are struggling, simply to report a good day.

It is remarkable how valuable a call home can be when one intuits that something is slightly out of kilter with a student. Parents sometimes fail to recognize that what is happening at home (death of a grandparent, father's loss of job, parent separation) takes a toll at school. Or they simply don't know how or to whom to report the news. Rarely is a parent anything but appreciative that the school is attuned to the child's needs and disposed to be supportive.

It takes time to call parents, and often teachers will avoid reporting troublesome news, assuming that a parent will respond negatively. In fact, appreciation from parents, even for a difficult call, far outweighs the negative response of those who feel inclined to punish the messenger. More often than not, the parent is seeing similar patterns at home and is eager to conspire with the school. Perhaps the only time that I find I cannot support a faculty member against an irate parent is if that teacher failed to communicate with a parent when the child first began to slide.

As the cost of an independent education spirals upwards, what parents are paying for primarily is to know what is happening in school. Good communication includes gently—or firmly, if necessary—steering a family toward outside professional help, if need be, remembering our responsibility to maintain an environment which is healthy for both individuals and the community at large.

A common mistake among schools who care is to spend so much time and effort on a child who presents singular challenges that they neglect those who are generally better balanced. I know I need to realign my priorities if parents voice concern that their child is not receiving enough attention because he or she is a good, quiet student, while somebody else in the class is outrageous enough to demand an inordinate amount of everyone's focus.

At Langley all middle school faculty are required to enter their phone conversations in an on-going log in my office. Emerging patterns are quickly identified, both by teachers and me, giving individual members the support of each other, and the connections make that element of my homework that much easier. Not only do I see who is making what calls and which children are needing extra attention, but I can also observe who is not communicating with parents and follow up with those individuals.

Parent Education

Parents of adolescents, especially, often benefit from regular instruction and guidance in how to parent. This generation of parents looks to the "experts" (us) for how-to advice. Wise schools implement programs which provide support for parents as they navigate their way through dual careers and a society whose sign posts are often obscured or confusing. Many schools utilize parent peer groups and/or make a point of bringing speakers to campus.

An area in which I suspect we can all improve is to approach the onslaught of adolescence much more proactively. Good schools are beginning to establish lecture/discussion series which cover topics from physical and emotional development in adolescence to chronic homework problems to the school's philosophy of grouping to informal discussions describing what parents should expect in the year to come. Parents are especially responsive to sessions dedicated to establishing general expectations for social activities outside of school. Most importantly, parents need to feel that their child's school is wise and experienced in areas in which they are not, and time and money spent in this area of PR and education are invaluable. Support groups for parents of middle school children defuse all kinds of misperceptions and anxieties.

Transitions

If the goal of a good middle school is to prepare its students for upper school, there must be some means of assessing its program. Establishing open communication with secondary schools in the case of schools which end after 8th grade, or developing formalized communication procedures with a school's own upper level should be a priority.

Equally important is the feedback of former students. I have found it most helpful to send a questionnaire to all recent graduates at the end of their first quarter of ninth grade. I ask them about their preparation in specific areas of the curriculum as well as query them about more amorphous things such as test preparation and willingness to take risks. Final questions are open-ended and designed to elicit responses to things about which they feel strongly. Middle school students are nothing if not honest, and I believe I get a fairly accurate reading of their experiences at Langley—as long as I remember to factor in the passion element.

Professional Development

Opportunities for professional development specific to middle school education abound, are critical to the educational process, and often are too expensive for small independent schools. Three division heads from schools within The Association of Independent Schools of Greater Washington established a Middle Schools Steering Committee six years ago. The Committee is open to any interested division heads. We meet quarterly to plan workshops for local middle school faculty and administrators and usually present two or three a year. Successful topics have included: Scheduling for the Middle School, Working with Learning Disabilities, The Impact of ADA, Math in the Middle, and Close Encounters of the Difficult Kind (role plays). We have also used the group to formulate guidelines for school dances. Attendance has been excellent and the workshops provide a forum for healthy and supportive exchange among colleagues. Occasionally we import an outside expert, but we believe it is more important, sometimes more valuable—and certainly cheaper—to turn to the considerable wisdom within our own ranks.

The role of workshop as support group is invaluable. Participants return to their own schools renewed and ready once again for battle, comforted by the fact that other middle school personnel are wrangling with the same challenges. Yes, we are a little bit crazy, but what we do is vital, and we do it in such good company.

20

On Virginity: Notes to Parents and Teachers

by Patrick F. Bassett, President
Independent Schools Association of the Central States

The idea of virginity, once sacred and fundamental to civilization, has become sullied to such an extent that the notion itself, at least in some "progressive" circles, is seen as a quaint anachronism, somewhat akin to good spelling and proper grammar: something more honored in the breach than in the practice. The Virgin Mary has been superseded in popular attention and reverence by Madonna, whose "Like a Virgin" song and whose stage persona represent the antithesis of the icon of The Virgin. The fact of virginity, however, is another matter: the most recent polls of adolescents show that around 50% of girls 17 and under (and slightly fewer boys) remain virgins (MacDonald, 74), resisting successfully the most powerful of pressures to join the crowd. Contrary to peer pressure ("Everyone is doing it"), popular media (Doogie Howser, Roseanne's daughter Becky, and Beverly Hills 90210's Brenda all lost their virginity this autumn's television season), the increasingly early onset of puberty itself, and decreasing adult disapproval of teen sexual experimentation, about half the teenagers on the block are holding out. Schools have complicated the matrix by a stance of basic moral cowardice: "We teach sex education, but we do not impose values here," a stance that is analogous to charting the course and rigging the boat, then merely hoping the child will refrain from launching prematurely. Despite the basic complicity and moral lassitude of most of the adult world, about half the teens have better sense than we do, perhaps knowing intuitively that preserving one's virginity, at least until adulthood if not until marriage, may be the safe and prudent route to take, since those who engage in sex prematurely are more often than not hurt in some way. This essay is intended to help the parents and teachers of the world to support the wise choice of virginity on the part of half the teens out there, and perhaps to change the trend line back to where it was way back when. . . . We can only be responsible if we address all three points along the continuum of advice to teens on sex: proselytize abstinence, counsel postponement, teach prevention. Some folks are telling teens that sex is unsafe (and kids don't believe it, at least for them); what we should be telling teens and what they should be hearing is that sex is unwise, until one is an adult.

The idea of virginity and chastity has been so deeply embedded in our civilization historically, mythically, and culturally that one should hesitate more pronouncedly than most apparently do at the current pronouncements about the demise of virginity. To paraphrase W.C. Fields, "The announcement of the death (of virginity) may be premature." At the very least, such a pronouncement should be judged unwise and unfortunate because, in part, it runs so counter to the accumulated mythical weight of the culture. For western culture, the archetypal virgin comes from both Greek and Christian heritages: for the Greeks, the ideal of virginity was embodied in both goddess (the demure Diana) and woman (Leda). In the case of Greek mythology, the violation of the virgin by the rape of Leda by Zeus in the form of a swan results in the birth of Helen, and ultimately the downfall of Troy. For Christians, the archetypal female virgin figure is of course Mary, Mother of God, and the archetypal male virgin figure is her son, Christ. Interestingly, the sacrifice of the virgin (Christ) in this case is the male rather than the female, a sacrificial death of the virgin (the pure and innocent) that is traceable almost universally not only to Greek and Christian heritages but also to to primitive and pagan cultures long before its enshrinement in Christian Gospel. Likewise, it is the male virgin in Arthurian legends who is ennobled and beatified, the Sir Galahad who succeeds in the search for the Holy Grail after Lancelot, compromised and no longer the virgin (no longer the Christ figure) fails. In English tradition, the power of the virgin finally became politically enshrined in Elizabeth, the Virgin Queen, lionized in literature as Edmund Spenser's *Faerie Queen.*

In contrast, it is the seduction, traducement, and despoilment of the virgin that our collective cultural and psychological heritage tells us is the most grievous of sins. From the Satan/serpent's seduction of Eve and the postlapsarial consequences of the Fall, we have embedded in our ancient stories the suggestion of horrible consequence for sexual transgression (i.e., sex outside of marriage). Freud's classical horrific image is the

Medusa's head, with its phallic snakes and sublimated suggestion of the punishment of castration for sexual sin. The idea of terrible punishment in the form of physical disfigurement for sexual sin is traceable from Classical drama (*Oedipus Rex*, in which Oedipus tears out his eyes upon discovering he has slept with his own mother), to Biblical narrative (Sodom and Gomorrah), through fairy tale and Gothic horror story into more contemporary popular art. In fairy tales, for example, it is clear that the psychological subtext of many stories is the admonishment to children that it is dangerous to entertain sexual encounters at a premature age. In the Brothers Grimm version of ''Little Red Cap'' (known to us now as ''Little Red Riding Hood''), it is clear that the wolf represents the animal/Id side of rapacious man, and the wolf's ''seduction'' of Little Red Cap to leave the path to play in the flowers (after mother had given strict orders to her to stay on the path to grandmother's) leads to her demise, in bed, at the mouth of the voracious wolf. Likewise, in ''Rapunzel,'' the mother/witch incarcerates Rapunzel at age 12, the age of puberty, in an inaccessible, doorless (phallic) tower. When Rapunzel ''unbound her braided tresses, opened the window, and let her hair down'' (all, incidentally, images of opening up and letting go), the prince spies the witch climbing up Rapunzel's hair, and he soon thereafter follows suit. In effect, the prince convinces Rapunzel to ride away with him on his horse (i.e., he seduces her), but before they can leave, the immature and naive Rapunzel tells the witch, who in turns punishes Rapunzel by cutting her hair (physical disfigurement). Subsequently the witch punishes the prince by casting him out of the tower, where he falls into the brambles which scratch his eyes into blindness (the classical Oedipal punishment for sexual transgression). It is only years later, after both wander in the sterile desert, that the prince again encounters Rapunzel; her tears fall on his eyes, restoring his sight, and they then marry happily: i.e., after enough time has passed so that Rapunzel is past childhood and ready for womanhood.

The defining event in all of the genre of horror is a monster's abduction of the virgin bride on the eve of her wedding. What makes the genre so horrific (and paradoxically so engaging and titillating) is the victimization of the virgin. Consider Bram Stoker's *Dracula*, Mary Shelley's *Frankenstein*, Robert Louis Stevenson's *Dr. Jekyll and Mr. Hyde*, and Gaston Leroux's *The Phantom of the Opera*: in each and every case, the monster has a grotesque deformity, a physical correlative for the bestial side of man, the Id's outcropping when unchecked by the civilizing effect of the Superego. One could also argue that within the physical deformity, especially the phallic imagery of the vampire's teeth drawing the virgin's blood, the stake through the neck (Frankenstein) or heart (Dracula), the missing nose (the original Phantom), the grossly disfigured face (Mr. Hyde), one sees that the Oedipal theme of terrible disfigurement as punishment for sexual transgression manifests itself time and again.

In more contemporary popular culture the idea of the virgin manifests itself still, although in much more complex forms, through the image of the Madonna/whore. It is arguable that the Madonna/whore image, the notion of the pure virgin and the "fallen woman," emerges in Christian gospel: the contrast between the two Marys, the Virgin Mary (Mary as virgin and virgin as mother) and the other Mary, Mary Magdalene, the whore who is resurrected through the intervention of Jesus. The rock star Madonna ("Like a Virgin"), who projects ponytailed innocence one moment and salacious experience the next, reflects just such a contemporary version of the Madonna/whore nexus. As another quintessential American popular genre indicates, the western, we have highly ambivalent attitudes at times about women, in fact, ambivalence about both the virgin and whore projections of woman. In the western, for example, the stock characters include the saloon girl and the school teacher. (In the forties and fifties classic westerns, the saloon girls were almost always part Mexican or part Indian, incidentally, and the virgins almost always white—see *Stagecoach*, *My Darling Clementine*, etc.) Invariably, the western hero sleeps with the saloon girl (and is closest to her of all other characters, sharing her wild, "untamed" nature) and is moved to action in the name of the school teacher but to protect the person of the saloon girl: it is either a direct or indirect threat from the bandits or the Indians towards the town or the wagon train (and specifically the young women living therein—i.e., the saloon girl and the virgin in white)—that propels the western hero, reluctantly, into the use of violence to restore order. The classic example of this is *High Noon*, where the sheriff (the Gregory Peck character) has to vanquish the bandits (the leader brandishing a terrible scar, monster-like) to protect the town, and by extension both the saloon girl (Helen Ramirez) and his virgin bride, literally dressed in white the entire time of the film (the Grace Kelly character). The tremendously powerful attraction of the film, as with the horror stories cited above, is connected to our collective need to experience vicariously the threat to the virgin while at the same time seeing that the threats to the principle of purity itself are ultimately vanquished, and terribly so in some cataclysmic retribution.

And so it goes with story after story that we continue to tell ourselves. Just as Freud argues that there must be something so powerful about the

Oedipus story to have made it popular for thousands of years (i.e., our unconscious sexual urges), so too one might argue is the case for stories of virginity, both the stories that affirm male and female virginity and those that take delight in repressing the figures who threaten it. If we have been telling ourselves these stories for so long, we might pause before we cast aside the ideal that they affirm: maintaining one's virginity until the sanctioned moment arrives, in adulthood and preferably under the blessing of marriage. Freud's basic thesis in *Civilization and Its Discontents* is that is it the displacement and sublimation of the Id's sexual energies by the Ego into one's work that produces great art and the conventions of civil life itself. Robert Coles, Harvard psychiatrist and professor, has argued that there may be some validation of Freud's theory in the research on teenage sexual activity: of those who plan to finish only "some of high school," 76% are nonvirgins; of those who plan to complete "all of college," 76% are virgins, the mirror opposite in numbers (Coles and Stokes, 203). We may well assume that the premature forsaking of virginity carries with it many dangers, personally, psychologically, societally. That is why we have been telling these stories about virgins for so long, and why our not listening to them now is so very dangerous.

The culture indeed has affirmed and deified virginity since humans became human, that is, since civilization took form, but the bombardment of images in the popular culture today are surely more weighted towards forsaking virginity for pleasure, *carpe diem*, than for restraining oneself until adulthood or marriage. It is somewhat surprising and reassuring, consequently, to find a significant number of adolescents who maintain their virginity, despite considerable pressure to do otherwise. The most recent polls indicate that around 50% of those 17 or younger remain virgins. Given the ease with which many teens (about half the group) engage in sexual activities, one might assume that not all of the rest are virgins out of necessity rather than choice. It is easy to assert cynically the unavailability of sexual partners for the virgins in the group, but it is more likely that some decision-making is going on that inclines this group not to look too hard for the partner willing to go the whole remaining 90 yards of the game. Once past seventeen, however, the figures change dramatically in the wrong direction. Seventy-two percent of high school seniors, male and female, have experienced sexual intercourse (according to the Centers for Disease Control), but those that hold out until that point seem to have made a firm decision to remain chaste, since 25 percent of females still remain virgins at 19 (and twenty percent of never-married women remain chaste through their twenties, as reported by The Alan Guttmacher

Institute) (Pagnozzi, 235). Since the physical, emotional, and psychological dangers of early intercourse increase as one goes down the age scale (the younger one starts, the more likely one is to have multiple partners and increased risks), our efforts as parents and teachers should be to work as vigorously on counseling postponement as we proselytize abstinence: the numbers show us that there are teens who make the abstinence or postponement choices, and we should exert our efforts to affirm their decisions and to make their numbers grow.

If there are fundamental cultural, moral, and parental prohibitions against premature engagement in sexual intercourse, then what are the countervailing pressures that teenagers feel that override the inhibitors? Current popular media are of course one source of powerful persuaders. The advertising world (Calvin Klein ads in particular), television soaps, sitcoms, and the film industry present sex without commitment and consequence in highly telescoped relations in which there is a collapsing into a short period of relationships that go from encounter to intercourse in the blink of a camera's eye. Many teenagers, when asked, indicate they believe that television and movies present realistic relationships. (One recent study revealed the naivete of the age when over half of the teenagers polled indicated that the way sex and its consequences are shown on television is the way it is in real life) (Howard, 75–6). Students who believe TV accounts of sex are accurate are more likely to be dissatisfied with their own first experiences (Haffner & Kelly, 31).

Peer pressure is possibly the most potent contributor to premature sexual involvement: many studies show that significant numbers of adolescents have engaged in intercourse not because they themselves wanted to but because they felt their partner expected it of them, and they did not know how to refuse (Howard, 75–6). In today's entertainment landscape the question of whether or not to engage in teen sex is merely rhetorical (O'Connor, 15). Furthermore, the fictional presentation of the stages of sex leave out crucial intervening steps: Doogie and Wanda in the TV sitcom "Doogie Howser, M.D." agonize for a polite period of time over the question of intercourse, kiss, grab the condoms (Doogie is a physician, after all, and safe sex is politically correct for the networks, if virginity is not), and jump into bed, giving the impression that seems universally assumed by too many teenagers: 1. That if there is a moral dimension to sexual intimacy, just hesitating is enough to show one's moral strength; 2. That if I do make a thoughtful decision to have sex, I will also be responsible and protect myself (while statistics show that most teen sex is spontaneous, and only 50% or less of it accompanied by precautionary measures to prevent pregnancy or disease); 3. That the natural successor to kissing is intercourse. How far we have traveled from the fictional landscape of the 1960 film *Where the Boys Are* (a film from the teen years of the current baby boomers and parents generation), a story in which the college girls on spring break in Florida actually resisted the temptations, with the notable exception of the Yvette Mimieux character, whose resulting pregnancy and demise is the cornerstone of the drama.

Schools are guilty, with parents, in not sending the signals needed to be sent to deliver the message that virginity is not only acceptable but preferable to the alternative. Research shows that although students actually prefer learning about sex from parents (first choice) and teachers (second choice), they in fact learn most from peers and the media (both highly unreliable and unrealistic sources). The crux of the problem with parents is an unwillingness to discuss the issues: only 10% of parents do, beyond just saying "Don't" (Rodman, Lewis, & Griffith, 70). The crux of the problem in schools lies in two phenomena: the unwillingness of academic faculties to address the issue and come to some consensus on it in the first place, and the substitution of sex education for moral education on the topic of human sexuality. It is rare to find a student handbook that actually proscribes sexual activities: schools are very clear on what to wear (dress codes) but shrink from suggesting not to undress. We can agree that smoking, drinking, and drugs are harmful and dutifully proscribe those behaviors but are confounded when we attempt to find common ground to set standards on teen sexual behaviors, largely because there is a generational disagreement between the younger teachers, themselves products of the sexual revolution of the sixties and seventies, and their more senior colleagues, whose experience with the revolution consists primarily in either helpless acquiescence or quiet revulsion over its path. Thus, the first order of business for schools is for the adults to meet and to fight it out· to say clearly and unequivocally what the standard will be within the schools for acceptable sexual behaviors and to agree what is prudent counseling for individual teachers to give to students who seek advice on the issues of sexuality. For us to reverse the trend of increasing sexual activity among teens, we must return to the point in which schools, parents, and the other moral authorities within the universe of children agree to proselytize abstinence, counsel postponement, and teach prevention. If we tilt our influence toward the first two points of the spectrum, then perhaps in more cases our instruction on the third point will be gratuitous.

It is with instruction on the third point, prevention of pregnancy and STDs (sexually transmitted diseases), that schools flounder time and again because of the misguided notion that a values-neutral approach to sex education is in fact neutral. On the contrary, the effect of what we do in sex education in most school programs is to teach the mechanics of human sexuality without the necessary admonishments about not turning on the engine so that the implicit message is that because one is of legal age to drive, it is fine to take the car around the block. Although few would argue that we should return to the days of general ignorance about human sexuality, increased familiarity with the mechanics of sexuality has demystified sex to the point of making it commonplace and, therefore, acceptable in the minds of most teenagers. We know that education alone is not enough to prevent teens from practicing dangerous and unhealthful activities: the anti-smoking campaign in schools has been comprehensive, so much so that everyone knows that cigarette smoking is deleterious to one's health (and in fact knows that at least from the second grade on). So why is it that the only subgroup of Americans increasing in the use of cigarettes is the adolescent female population? Because peer pressure and meretricious advertising both conspire to suggest that smoking is "cool" and "adult," even somewhat "racy" (The Virginia Slims'—"You've Come a Long Way, Baby"—modern woman, and Camel's swanky—camel—modern male, are attractive icons for kids). Likewise with sex education: education is not the issue, anymore, since we have successfully inundated kids with warnings about teenage pregnancy, and STDs, especially AIDS. For the most part, kids know how pregnancy occurs and know the precautions one should take to prevent adverse health consequences. The problem, of course, is that knowledge is not the issue so much as values and decision-making patterns. One might use the alcohol and drug education campaigns to illustrate the point: we tried to educate until we were blue in the face regarding the dangers of adolescent use of alcohol and drugs, but the most effective deterrents were to legislate an older drinking age (18 to 21) and to hold parents, schools, colleges, and universities legally responsible for the Dionysian excesses commonly experienced when teenagers use alcohol or other drugs. At that point, parents and schools began campaigns to change adolescent attitudes and decision-making so that the "I choose not to use" attitude became acceptable. The surprising development of smoke-free and alcohol-free dormitories to choose on an increasing number of campuses reveals the salubrious effect of the shift in attitudes on alcohol and drugs. (Incidentally, one might recommend to teenagers on the subject of use of alcohol the same epigram as for early sexual encounters: to proselytize absti-nence, counsel postponement, and teach prevention—of alcoholism, in this case). Unfortunately, just the opposite movement in the schools is taking place in the case of developing attitudes towards early sexual activity: rather than discourage early activity, we implicitly and explicitly encourage it by providing condoms to children. It is with shock that some parents moving their daughters into the coed dorm in which they will live their freshmen year discover that in the concession area, one can purchase condoms from what used to be the cigarette machines. The messages are clear: don't smoke here, but grab a condom with your soft drink and bag of chips, to slake your appetite or to accompany your evening's enter-tainment. The AIDS epidemic, of course, has dramatized the urgency in the need to educate our children about the dangers of sexual encounters, but since only abstinence is completely safe, and since most teenage intercourse (between 50% and 90% according to different reports) is unprotected, we must realize that the health education argument falls largely on deaf ears.

What, then, is the good counsel parents and teachers should give to adolescents to help them make the choice of virginity?

First, that while we will teach prevention, we favor abstinence and counsel postponement. We might add that for those who have already made the plunge, it is not too late and indeed wise to become abstinent now: better late than never.

Second, that we believe that virginity should be preserved for adult-hood or marriage . . . depending on one's value system. Each of us would define adulthood differently: some by age (18 or 21), some by stage (out of high school and working or in college), some by level of independence ("You are not an adult until you pay your own way," or "the Golden Rule of parenting: he who holds the gold makes the rule"). Adults should be able to agree that adulthood never occurs at 17 or younger, since rare is the teen who is capable of making all the judgments necessary to handle the commitment and consequences of sex at an earlier age.

Third, that there is a hierarchy of expressions of caring and love, steps and stages that should be followed, and that there is no need to rush to intercourse . . . as the final step when there is plenty of time to arrive there eventually. Although parents and teachers often feel comfortable describ-ing and diagraming the most intimate of genitalia, (since an academic, distanced, clinical approach is non-threatening to all involved), it is the steps of intimacy that we avoid talking about and that need much further exploration by our children. An alumna of a former school of mine once told me that when she was permitted to have a male friend to school, she was only permitted to entertain him in the front parlor, under direct supervision from the headmistress. When her date became particularly adventurous and placed his hand over hers, the headmistress came over to whisper in her ear, "Don't you think you should save something for marriage?" We've come a long way indeed from that quaint attitude, but perhaps too long a way for anyone's well-being. Put more graphically for clarity's sake, there are ways of talking, touching, caring, sharing that are very intimate but fall short of invasive, penetrating sexuality, what we should be counseling our children to avoid.

Fourth, that to choose virginity is to take pride in oneself and to manifest strength of character, despite what others may say. One does not have to be a nerd "to choose not to use" alcohol or drugs, just as one does not have to be a prude to choose to abstain from sexual intercourse at too early an age. In fact, "The times, they are a-changing": there are encouraging signs that many students are choosing for a variety of reasons to abstain. Any friendship that is jeopardized by an abstinence choice needs repair in the first place.

It has been my experience and that of many of my colleagues that when an adolescent comes to an adult seeking counsel about sexual experimentation, what the adolescent is most often seeking are ways to say "No." If an adolescent wishes validation to experiment, he or she would go to a peer. The fact of an adolescent's seeking out an adult on this difficult issue demands an adult response. The ideal becomes to proselytize abstinence and teach postponement so that prevention becomes a moot point. After all, *loss* of virginity is just that, a loss teens need not contend with given the proper advice and the encouragement to develop their own strong will.

SOURCES AND RESOURCES

Burkhart, Kathryn Watterson. *Growing into Love.* New York: G.P. Putnam's Sons, 1981.

Coles, Robert and Geoffrey Stokes. *Sex and the American Teenager.* New York: Harper's, 1885.

Francoeur, Robert T., Ed. *Taking Sides: Clashing Views on Controversial Issues in Human Sexuality.* Guilford, CT: The Dushkin Publishing Group, 1989.

Haffner, Debra and Marcy Kelly, "Adolescent Sexuality in the Media." SIECUS Report, March/April 1987. Excerpted in "Teenage Sexuality. Opposing Viewpoints", David L. Bender and Bruno Leone, Series Editors. St. Paul, MN: Greenhaven Press, 1988.

Howard, Marion. *How to Help Your Teenager Postpone Sexual Involvement.* New York: The Continuum Publishing Co., 1991.

MacDonald, Donald Ian. "An Approach to the Problem of Teenage Pregnancy." *Public Health Reports*, July-August, 1987. Reprinted in "Teenage Sexuality. Opposing Viewpoints", David L. Bender and Bruno Leone, Series Editors. St. Paul, MN: Greenhaven Press, 1988.

O'Connor, John J. "Critics Notebook: On Teen-age Virginity, or Its Loss, On TV." *New York Times*, 09/25/91.

Orr, Lisa, editor. *Sexual Values: Opposing Viewpoints.* San Diego, CA: Greenhaven Press, 1989.

Pagnozzi, Amy. "Virgin With Attitude." *Glamour*, April, 1992.

Rodman, Hyman, Susan H. Lewis, and Saralyn B. Griffith. *The Sexual Rights of Adolescents.* New York: Columbia University Press, 1984. Excerpted in "Teenage Sexuality, Opposing Viewpoints", David L. Bender and Bruno Leone, Series Editors. St. Paul, MN: Greenhaven Press, 1988.

21

The Road to
Drug-Free Schools

by Richard A. Hawley, Head of School
University School, Hunting Valley

When he was elected to the Presidency in 1988, George Bush expressed the hope that he would come to be regarded as the "education president." Toward this end his administration formulated a program of six goals that, if achieved, would result in globally competitive and otherwise excellent schools by the century's end.

The sixth goal of the President's plan was stated as follows: "By the year 2,000, every school in America will be free of drugs and violence and will offer a disciplined environment conducive to learning." Underlying this intention was the growing conviction that improved learning outcomes would have to be preceded by the establishment of a school culture in which teaching and learning could effectively be carried out. This conviction was not limited to political conservatives such as former

---

[1]"Monitoring the Future" is a 15-year, running survey, by Lloyd D. Johnston, Patrick M. O'Malley, and Jerald G. Bachman, of approximately 17,000 high school seniors (and more recently college students and other young adults) from public and private schools in every region of the country. The study's findings are drawn from self-reporting questionnaires administered in the schools by the research team. The research has been carried out under the auspices of the University of Michigan Institute for Social Research, supported by a series of grants from the National Institute on Drug Abuse (NIDA). A report by Johnston, O'Malley, and Bachman titled "Drug Use, Drinking, and Smoking: National Survey Results from High School, College, and Young Adults Populations, 1975–1988" (Rockville, MD.: NIDA, 1989), is available from NIDA, 5600 Fishers Lane, Rockville, MD 20857.

Education Secretary William Bennett who, as Bush's appointed "drug czar," would be largely responsible for initiating programs to realize Goal Six. By the late '80s, even former education "radicals" like Neil Postman would state firmly in his *Teaching as a Conserving Activity* that an essential precondition for learning is a safe, orderly, and respectful learning environment.

As the Bush administration began its work, there were some encouraging signs of progress in the direction of drug-free schools. According to the best and most long-standing survey of drug use among the nation's high school students, conducted by Lloyd Johnston, Patrick O'Malley, and Jerald Bachman[1], the level of drug use in general was showing signs of decline. Moreover, 1989 figures showed that the use of certain substances—marijuana and powder cocaine, in particular—was down significantly.

These encouraging findings require some qualification, however. The national high school survey does not include the 15% to 20% of high schoolers who drop out, a population especially "at risk" for drug abuse. And while the survey breaks down patterns of drug use by region, it is not structured to provide information to answer the questions school officials would most like answered: Do a school's concerted efforts to create a drug-free environment produce measurable, visible results? Or do vaguer out-of-school factors shape the drug scene?

As the Clinton administration begins to shape its own drug and education policies, it is time to take stock again, especially as there are indications of a renewed interest in drugs on the part of school-aged users. Even the documented decline in certain forms of youthful drug use in 1989 was no cause for excessive optimism. The new, lower levels of use were still destructively high. Forty-four percent of high school seniors reported having tried marijuana; fifteen years previously, the reported percentage was about the same, 47%. In 1975, 9% of the seniors surveyed reported having at least tried cocaine; fifteen years later the figure was over 10%. In 1989, about three out of a hundred seniors reported having used cocaine during the previous month; about 17 out of a hundred reported having used marijuana. Distributed evenly throughout a school, these figures suggest that five or six students in each classroom might be drug impaired; the same might be said of two starters on the varsity football team, several members of the cast and crew of the school musical, and so on. Toss into the mix the fact that one in three students reports having been drunk (five or more drinks in a row) over the past two weeks, and you are not even within screaming distance of a drug-free school.

Some History

The public, including the nation's students, has grown inured to the idea of "the drug problem." There is the wearying impression that we have heard all the cautionary lessons before. For the current generation of children, there has "always been" a drug problem. But the fact of the matter is that there hasn't always been a drug problem, at least not in American schools.

Drug-addled children and drug-riddled schools are a phenomenon of the late 20th century. Prior to 1964, drug use by school-age children was negligible to nonexistent in the literature of pediatric medicine, public health, law enforcement, and education policy. Within a decade, youthful drug use was epidemic, possibly the most distinctive feature of the rise of the counterculture.

Profound spiritual and political explanations have been advanced to account for the growth of the youth culture of the Sixties and Seventies, but perhaps the most persuasive explanation has to do with the sheer number of postwar baby boomers who entered adolescence between 1965 and 1974. Whole complexes of social life—suburbs and malls—were erected to house them and provide for their needs. New, streamlined schools were constructed; later, mega-universities were expanded to accommodate enrollments by an influx of baby boomers. For several consecutive years there were more Americans under than over 25 years of age.

This mass of youth grew up in conditions of unprecedented affluence and mobility. Expressed on such a scale, the ordinary tension between adolescents and the adult order felt ominous and system-threatening. Hair grew long, conventions of dress changed dramatically, new looks and new voices dominated the popular culture. This new youth-driven culture said yes to spontaneity, impulsiveness, and sensuality; it said no to discipline, tradition, and moderation. The media, captivated by so much novelty, tended to impute certain ephemeral countercultural attitudes— for example, "Make Love Not War"—to the young generally. But only in the media did the youth of America grow ideologically radical. In 1968, the first year in which 18-year-olds were able to vote in a Presidential election, they cast their votes predominantly for the Republican candidate, Richard Nixon. In fact, they supported him more strongly than their parents did.

By the late Seventies, the counterculture generation began to abandon the outward trappings of adolescence and became more conventional, more conservative, and, the critics claimed, more self-centered. This change might be called the birth of the "me generation." But while long hair, bell-bottomed trousers, and ideological slogans were quickly abandoned, the production, distribution, and use of psychoactive drugs was left firmly and massively in place, especially among school-age children.

Because drugs act on and alter the nervous system, they cannot be discarded along with Nehru jackets and love beads. Drug use is not merely a matter of attitude or style. Only when children make a "threshold" choice to try a drug can they be said to deliberate objectively. Once the drug has interacted with the nervous system—including perhaps an overwhelming neurochemical discharge of pleasurable sensations—the drug's effect becomes part of all subsequent deliberations. When a person proceeds from casual use to dependency, the drug becomes the primary determinant of decision-making. The young people of the counterculture tended to abandon many of their one-time preferences, but the use of illegal drugs persisted.

Illicit drug use among children reached peak levels between 1978 and 1980. In 1978 and 1979, for example, more than one high school senior in 10 reported using marijuana daily. By this time, the public manifestation of the problem could no longer be ignored. Research scientists and physicians began to make an unambiguous case against the use of psychoactive drugs, especially marijuana, which had previously been represented by advocates as a relatively mild intoxicant.

The public momentum away from "recreational" drug use and away from drug use of any kind by children began in the mid-Seventies with a passionate but loosely organized collection of grassroots gestures. Research scientists, such as anesthesiologist Gabriel Nahas and pharmacologist Carlton Turner, were invited to an informal annual conference in Atlanta to explore approaches to stemming the burgeoning epidemic of drug use. These early Parents Resources In Drug Education (PRIDE) conferences were conceived and chartered by a Georgia State University physical education professor, Thomas Gleaton, and an Atlanta parent and doctoral candidate in English literature, Marsha Manatt Schuchard. By the late Seventies the PRIDE organization was drawing in national authorities on the prevention of drug abuse.

PRIDE also captured the attention of the White House drug advisors, the U.S. Congress, the armed services—and especially of schools, including their parent/teacher associations. By the early Eighties the PRIDE organization had become international in scope, and its annual conference came to include the U.S. attorney general, First Lady Nancy Reagan, and celebrities and entertainers opposed to drug use.

Only a few Americans are likely to know or care much about the origins of the PRIDE organization, but it is worth noting that PRIDE began as an expression of educational and parental concern about drug-related losses among schoolchildren. Its earliest support came from an eclectic group of scientists and intellectuals, men and women who shared no particular political agenda. A movement later labeled as "conservative" and "right wing" by pro-drug lobbyists and by *Playboy* was in fact launched by independent progressives during the Carter Administration. It is this movement to which Nancy Reagan and the slogan "Just Say No" became affixed in the Eighties. The first lady discovered and embraced the antidrug crusade; she did not by any means create it.

Lingering Dissonance

The effects of pleasure-inducing toxic chemicals—i.e., drugs—on the human nervous system and the ensuing effects on behavior are so complex that it is hard to describe them simply and clearly. Cannabis alone is composed of hundreds of biological substances. The nervous system is composed of billions of neurons and even more neural connections. So much complexity and subtlety does not lend itself readily to bumper-sticker epigrams. However, all things considered, "Just Say No" isn't a bad start.

In an open society, firm policy and behavior-directing norms follow from a strong social consensus. For example, there is now a strong social consensus that people who behave in odd ways should not be labeled as witches, and, even if that label is applied, those so designated should not be burned. This consensus was a long time coming. While it might be demonstrated that recent progress has been made in restoring a social consensus that drug use is harmful to healthy human functioning, a number of obstacles are slowing the momentum.

That specialized knowledge is required to understand drug-related pathologies and losses has already been noted. However, misunderstanding also results from the inherent inability of even very intelligent non-addicts to understand the phenomenon of addiction or drug dependency. Non-addicts feel in control of their choices and decisions. They know they could pass up an opportunity to use an intoxicating substance. Non-addicts project this assumed control onto others, including addicts. They are likely to ask, How could a person drink or smoke crack cocaine on the job? The non-addict has no experience of losing control of decision-making. The addict asks the opposite question: How could a person pass up an opportunity for intoxication?

Non-addicts frequently respond to drug-related issues in one of two equally problematic ways. "Conservatives" may want to blame or punish the addict for making destructive choices, an approach that is ultimately futile because, with respect to drugs, an addict has no choice. "Liberals" are inclined to believe that informed choices can be made about drugs and that only destructive behavior, not mere drug use, should be proscribed. Liberals do not understand the casual, frequently one-way relationship between drug use, loss of decision-making, and destructive behavior. Confronted with actual addicts or with data documenting destructive behavior, many liberals tend to blame a repressive system that reduces people to such miserable circumstances that drugs are a freely chosen, though destructive, alternative to those circumstances.

Drug use is reinforced by a more powerful (and more toxic) neurological "reward" than that derived from other forms of delinquency, such as vandalism or shoplifting. Drug use is thus built more deeply and permanently into behavior. Addicts know this; non-addicts usually do not. Still, most people are not addicts, and it is this majority that establishes the norms regulating the use of drugs.

A related misunderstanding adds further confusion to drug-related decision-making: a rhetorical emphasis on the civil rights and civil liberties of drug takers and would-be drug takers. There is no constitutional or other traditional right safeguarding the production, distribution, or use of drugs. Intoxicants have been openly regulated—and, in many instances, prohibited—throughout the history of civilization. New knowledge about some intoxicants—e.g., cocaine—has altered policy and attitudes, just as knowledge about alleged witches has altered policy and attitudes. But taking drugs has not historically been included among the protected human prerogatives: to speak freely, to worship as one chooses, to assemble, and to participate in public decision-making.

Theorists from Plato to Lawrence Kohlberg have suggested that the law—that is, what is deemed lawful—is for most children and many adults the highest ethical criterion. School children tend to back up decisions and arguments with references to what rules and laws say. Children are troubled and confused by perceived ambivalence about what is right and lawful: laws that are not enforced, laws violated by those assigned to uphold them, "expert" disagreement over the validity of laws.

Confusion and, ultimately, bad decisions result when children see signs outside a concert hall stating "No alcoholic beverages allowed" but then enter to find open drinking and drug taking. Youthful commitments to abstain from alcohol and drugs are undermined when a Supreme Court nominee or the mayor of the nation's capital or the President of the United States admits to drug use.

Arguments to legalize drugs run powerfully against the consensus that drugs are destructive to individuals and to society. The law has mandated that asbestos be removed speedily and at massive public and private expense because it is toxic. Drugs cause exponentially more deaths, pathology, and loss of productivity than asbestos does, yet prominent and "expert" voices periodically argue for their legalization. This is confusing.

Apart from undermining the conviction that drugs are bad for people, the notion of legalizing drugs is fraught with difficulties and contradictions. The appeal of legalization seems to lie in a strange conjunction of hedonism, frustration, and a brittle adherence to market economics. Proponents of legalization assume that, once drugs are legally available, drug-related crime will, by definition, be reduced or disappear. But in reality this is wildly unlikely, unless the government wants to vend and tax heroin, crack cocaine, "ice" (methamphetamine), LSD, and PCP along with Marlboros and Jack Daniels. Few legalization advocates want to see all drugs licensed and offered for sale. But unless that is what happens, the really potent stuff, the deadly stuff, will be produced and sold illegally.

Nationalizing and legitimizing an addictive vice may or may not alter courtroom traffic and prison occupancy, but it will certainly not alter the effects of toxic chemicals on the health and conduct of human beings. That is the real drug problem, not the legal status of suppliers and users. Advocates of legalization are remarkably silent about projected consequences.

What does history teach us? Alcohol and tobacco are regulated by the state and are legally available. Of the two, only alcohol is psychoactive enough to be meaningfully analogous to the current illicit drugs. Together or separately alcohol and tobacco cause a thousandfold more deaths and illnesses annually than all of the illicit drugs combined. Once more, alcohol and tobacco are less psychoactive than illicit drugs, they are legally regulated, and their use is embedded in long-standing social conventions. Still they are the greatest killers and debilitators. Should other, more potent toxins be added to the legal pantry? Historical experience suggests that legalization is a deadly idea.

Historical perspective is not emphasized much in drug policy deliberations. To the extent that the historical record is scanned at all, it tends to be scanned badly. The impact of drug saturation on highly developed cultures—cannabis on Moslem culture in the medieval centuries, opium on Chinese culture in the 19th century—has been all but ignored. The "lesson" of Prohibition has been read as the failure of a repressive, puritanical assault on a sturdy American convention, resulting in 14 years of booming organized crime.

In fact, Prohibition was the culmination of a populist, progressive reform movement that had been building in individual states for decades. It was a close cousin of the reforms that led to cleaning up the meat industry and to countless public health measures. Prohibition reflected the sentiments of a majority of the nation's women who, without votes, commercial credit, or access to professional credentials, felt that they had suffered too long, both physically and financially, at the hands of drunken men.

Whatever its obvious failures in design and execution, Prohibition did not exacerbate the nation's drinking problem, the problem it addressed. The consumption of alcohol and the incidence of alcohol-related disease declined markedly during Prohibition. Those problems have mounted steadily since its repeal. If the lesson of Prohibition is that it "didn't solve the problem," the lesson of repeal is that it "made the problem worse."

The current dissonance about the status of the nation's "drug problem" is an obstacle to building a consensus that children develop best in a drug-free climate, which includes drug-free schools. Drug advocates and opponents alike too often cast aside logic, evidence, and historical perspective in their zeal to carry a point.

Drugs and the Development of Children

Because intoxicating chemicals impair the healthy functioning of the nervous system and because the nervous system is the organ of learning, growing children should be drug-free. Maturing nervous systems are more critically impaired by intoxicants than mature ones; childhood losses in learning are lifelong and profound. Moreover, children grow chemically dependent more quickly than adults, and their record of recovery is depressingly poor.

Diagnosing and treating drug-impaired children is a necessary therapeutic gesture, but it is a woefully insufficient approach to the youthful drug problem. As Nahas told his PRIDE conferees and any others who would listen, "Medicalization" is not the solution. Unless the climate for experimenting with and using drugs is changed, medical treatment will become an appendage and support of the drug culture. A booming proliferation of drug-abuse professionals and new treatment centers is not, in the long run, good news.

If the solution to the drug problem is not medicalization, or at least not medicalization by itself, what is? The answer is to renorm society's response to illicit drug use. Here Johnston, O'Malley, and Bachman's findings offer some encouragement. Their surveys have found that growing numbers of high school students perceive that it is harmful to try or to use illicit drugs. For example, in 1975 about 18% of the students polled believed that occasional marijuana smoking posed a "great risk"; in 1989 more than twice as many perceived occasional marijuana use as a great risk. Also in 1989, 78% felt that smoking pot regularly is a great risk, and a similarly large majority (71%) perceived the occasional use of cocaine as a great risk. In 18 different drug categories, high school students have reported increasing concern annually about the harmfulness of experimentation and use.

Practically, the evidence suggests that both society at large and individual schools would do well to adopt a "systematic" approach to the prevention of drug abuse. In other words, the supply, distribution, and use of drugs should all be confronted. Educational programs, public health bulletins, and drug treatment should all be undertaken. The recent decline in youthful drug use seems attributable to a decline in demand—which, in turn, can be attributed principally to the effectiveness of cautionary educational programs and to a firmer, though still dissonant, social consensus that drugs are harmful. There have been fewer successes to report on the "supply" side, as whole nations are brutally terrorized by powerful drug traffickers. Synthetic "designer drugs," such as "ecstasy" (MDMA) or "ice" (methamphetamine) have also slipped into the marketplace over the past few years, though their use has not yet become epidemic among school-age children.

What the law says and does about drug trafficking and use will have a significant impact on the young. In addition to reducing the available supply of dangerous substances, antidrug laws and policy will resonate agreeably with early childhood cautions to avoid danger, to promote health, and to obey community rules.

Plato and Aristotle stressed that children must become practiced in life-enhancing, community-regarding behavior before they are educated to understand intellectually the value of such actions. This developmental necessity is too easily forgotten. Good habits precede understanding. Children must be enjoined to tell the truth before they understand the moral grounds for doing so. Without the initial habit, later intellectual understanding will be mere sophistry.

Schools must be prescriptive and descriptive about the "drug problem." But they must be prescriptive first. Trustees and headmasters and teachers must be in accord. Policy and practice must be in accord. They must be in accord that drug-involved children are destructive to themselves, potentially destructive to other children, and destructive of school business generally.

A clear consensus, firm policy, and decisive action will move the nation rapidly toward the goal of drug-free schools. Doing so requires little specialized knowledge and, really, no money at all. Primary emphasis should be placed on threshold decisions: decisions to try a dangerous substance for the first time. This means clear messages in elementary and middle school classrooms. Tobacco and alcohol have traditionally been the "gateway" drugs for children; they are followed by marijuana, inhalants, and household medicines—then the rest.

Independent schools are ideally structured to prescribe and to describe important health measures, and school children are invariably responsive, provided the matter at hand is real and tangible, not abstract and remote. Schools can no longer be said to lack the resources to confront youthful drug use. However, some of them do lack the will. Drug-free schools are possible by the year 2000. Many schools, especially religious schools, are substantially drug-free today. A systemic approach to the prevention of drug abuse, however, will require clear and forceful measures in other arenas as well: in the workplace, on the highways, in public spaces (parks, concert halls, sports stadiums), and in households. Progress in these arenas, too, will require a strong social consensus.

How badly do Americans want drug-free schools? How do they feel about the schools they have? If Johnston, O'Malley, and Bachman's findings for seniors apply to the American high school population at large, then the typical high school of a thousand students now enrolls 437 who will smoke pot, 103 who will try cocaine, 83 who will try LSD, and 13 who will use heroin. One hundred sixty-seven will have smoked pot recently, and 28 will have used cocaine recently. By the time they are seniors, more than 90% of the student body will have tried alcohol, 66%, will drink with some regularity, and one in three will be frequently drunk. Two hundred eighty-six students will smoke cigarettes, and 189 of them will smoke daily.

The drug-saturated years have been a worrisome, dismal period in the history of American schooling. What do we need to produce drug-free schools? What do we need to produce good schools? We need only the national will to do so. More immediately, we need school leaders, faculty and staff who are convinced that drug-free schools are necessary: men and women courageous enough to make those schools possible.

School Strategies that Work

American education is not enjoying a Golden Age. Many schools are drug-ridden, and this is exacting an educational toll. Nevertheless, drug use by young people is a problem that can be beaten. Schools have been drug-free in the still-recollectable past; they can be again. Indeed, many have already begun.

Some prescriptions follow for changing the drug climate in the schools. Let me say at the outset that the policies I propose are my own passionate preferences, but they also happen to coincide with the positions of the American Council for Drug Education, the National Federation of Parents, the Parents Resource Institute for Drug Education, and the Texans' War on Drugs, among other national and regional organizations.

1. The school's commitment must be to become drug-free. This is a basic premise and a value-laden choice. It generates one kind of policy and program; other premises—to cut down on the levels of drug use or to help students make "responsible" drug choices—lead to different policies and programs. Robert DuPont, one of the clearest voices in the field of drug abuse prevention, likes to tell school faculties, "Every school will have precisely the amount of drug use that it tolerates."

It is only a sign of the times that the goal of maintaining drug-free schools is sometimes challenged as "unrealistic." The very mission of universal education requires a drug-free atmosphere for learning. Practically every reader of this chapter is acquainted personally with a casualty, if not a fatality, resulting from drug use. Allowing such a state of affairs to exist is inhumane—and "unrealistic."

2. Leaders must endorse, articulate, and stand by a school's commitment to be drug-free. The responsibility for changing a school's drug climate should be widely shared, but it cannot be delegated. Especially in the early stages, a tough stand on drugs will involve confrontations, dispensing bad news, and taking criticism. If the "drug problem" becomes the special assignment of an assistant district superintendent or of a school's dean of students or of a special faculty task force, those people are likely to be seen as the district's or the school's drug fanatics, and school leaders will be asked to mitigate and temper drug policies that some may find uncomfortable. This is a mistake. Maintaining a disinterested stance and keeping a reasonable distance from the problem by delegating drug policy to others will seem the easier course to a school leader, but doing so is almost certain to impede the process of ridding schools of drugs.

3. *Preventing drug abuse is easier, more educational, and more fun than remediating drug problems once they exist.* Prevention, intervention, and treatment are all essential ingredients of anti-drug abuse policies, but prevention is by far the most promising approach. Unlike older, more stable drug abusers, adolescents pass from experimental drinking bouts to full-blown chemical dependencies in a matter of months. The news from the facilities that treat young drug dependents is frankly discouraging. The majority of those who have been treated lapse back into drug abuse. Even among those who persevere and remain drug-free, the reintegration into family, school, and community is not easy. Moreover, a newly described clinical syndrome, PDIS (Post Dependence Impairment Syndrome), suggests that recovering dependents show abnormally high tendencies to chronic illness, injuries, learning difficulties, and depression.

The long-term answer is to prevent drug abuse before it begins. Schools are most likely to succeed in achieving this aim if they allot more and better instructional time to drug education before children confront the choice of whether or not to use a threshold drug. This means installing programs in elementary schools. Some exercises will be effective: how to say no and how to avoid drug use and other harmful situations. Some lessons will be informational: what is safe and what is dangerous; what are the effects on the human system of various legal and illegal drugs. Special emphasis should be given to cigarettes, alcohol, marijuana, and inhalants, because these are the most prevalent threshold drugs.

However, even the best educational programs can be subverted by the absence of strong, clear institutional policies forbidding drug use. For the great majority of school-age children, adherence to the "rules" and observance of the law are the highest categories of ethical thought. Schools tend to stress the enforcement of those policies about which they care most strongly. Drug education must go hand in hand with an anti-drug policy.

Weary voices stating that "drug education" and "information" have proved ineffectual as ways of preventing drug abuse are misinformed and mistaken. A systematic, prevention-based program of drug education has barely begun nationwide. The drug epidemic arose in the absence of such educational measures, not despite them.

4. Changing the drug climate of a school begins with building a consensus among members of the faculty and staff. School staffs whose members are divided among themselves cannot stand firm against student drug use. They will be divided in the same way inconsistent parents are divided. Building a durable consensus is apt to require some learning on the part of faculty members about the bio-medical effects of drugs and about their special effects on developing children. This learning may require some high-quality in-service training. The trainers and the materials they use should endorse the goal of a drug-free school. The entire faculty and staff (K-12) of a school system should be included in policy-making and program-building. Drug education is not the special business of health teachers and science teachers. The support of coaches and advisors is especially crucial to an effective school or system-wide drug policy.

5. Faculty members and staff members must restrict their own behavior to what is lawful and consistent with effective performance. Employee Assistance Programs (EAPs) for faculty and staff members with drinking and other drug problems are increasingly common in both public and private schools. Adults who have been treated through EAPs and who have remained in their posts tend to bolster rather than undermine the overall morale of a school; at the same time, their presence underscores the school's commitment to be drug-free.

6. Drug-free means alcohol-free. Alcohol is the principal drug of abuse among U.S. school children. It is the preferred drug of the majority of chemical dependents, and its use is more likely than any other disease, accident, or activity to lead to the violent death of young people. School faculty members must be educated to respond to the standard defenses for and denials of underage drinking: How much harm is there in a little? I don't want my son or daughter going off to college inexperienced. Well, if they're going to drink, I at least want them to do it here where I can watch them. Hell, I used to throw back a few myself. At least it's only alcohol. At least it's only beer.

Alcohol is the problem, not the form in which it is taken. A can of beer, a typical glass of wine, and a Scotch and soda served at a bar each contains about an ounce of alcohol. Two consecutive ounces of alcohol consumed by a five-year-old can kill the child. The same dose is highly toxic to a middle-schooler. Growing children are in the process of developing controls that might allow them to drink moderately as adults; alcohol and other drugs replace these controls. The loss of performance, health and life of young drinkers is well-documented and obvious. Against these losses, no positive benefits have been adduced.

Camaraderie? Fellowship? Go observe the middle-schoolers in the basement recreation room or the high school crowd at the rumored three-kegger at the home of a student whose parents are out of town. Observe, and perhaps clean up.

And now to work.

22

Meeting the Needs of Gay & Lesbian Students: A Plan of Action for Our Schools

by Kevin Jennings, Co-Chair of the Education Committee of Massachusetts Governor William Weld's Commission on Gay & Lesbian Youth; History Teacher, Concord Academy

I'm 17 and I'm gay. Adolescence is hell for me. I am told that my sexuality is something to be ashamed of, something to hide, something evil. I have cowered in my closet in shame and fear. I found myself lying to parents and friends, being constantly afraid of discovery, and censuring my words and actions with paranoid concentration. I remember hiding books from my parents because I was ashamed of them discovering about me. In short, I hated my sexuality and myself. My closet wasn't a refuge, it was a prison, and it was destroying me. By staying silent, I was confirming the emotions that were killing me inside. I am not just a statistic. I live in a Boston suburb in a white house with black shutters. I go to school everyday, feeling that I can't be honest, that I have no right to be proud, that I am a second-class citizen. Just this past week, as I was walking down my street in my town where I have lived all my life, a pick-up truck full of guys ran me off the road, screaming, "You lesbian!" at me. Homophobia is everywhere, and bigotry is inexcusable. It's time to start showing you care.
—Testimony of a seventeen-year-old lesbian student before the Massachusetts Governor's Commission on Gay & Lesbian Youth, November 1992.

As a History instructor in Concord, Massachusetts, I am well aware that I teach only a half-mile from where the American Revolution began at Concord's Old North Bridge. Having been born about two hundred years too late for that particular Revolution, I was pleased to be offered the chance to take part in another one when I was appointed Co-Chair of the Education Committee of Massachusetts Governor William Weld's Commission on Gay & Lesbian Youth in June, 1992. Building on growing concern about the needs of gay youth inspired by the reports of the high rate of suicide among this population, Governor Weld charged our Commission with investigating the problem and proposing concrete steps the state should take to alleviate the conditions that drove these youth to want to kill themselves. Since its creation, the Commission's work has helped to break new ground in serving a population which has traditionally been invisible in most of our schools.

Through a survey of scholarly literature, the Governor's Commission first identified the key problems that gay youth face. Public hearings, at which over one hundred youth and youth service providers spoke, were held throughout the state in November and December, 1992 to gather first-person evidence. The picture that emerged is an instructive one for all educators to study.

For those who are new to the issue, some background might be helpful. According to Professor James Sears of the University of South Carolina, the average student realizes his/her sexual orientation at age 13. For a heterosexual student, many avenues of support—family, friends, school, and community—exist to help with any difficulties that arise after this realization. By contrast, gay students rarely feel able to ask their families, friends, schools, or communities for help, fearing the possible response they might get. The essential difference between gay/lesbian youth and those youth from other under-represented populations (such as Jews, African-Americans, or Latinos) is that gay/lesbian youth do not grow up with people like themselves. The products of heterosexual families in the vast majority of cases, gay/lesbian youth usually come from communities where few gay/lesbian adults are visible, attend schools with no openly gay staff, and belong to friendship groups where "fag" is the favored insult and "that's so gay' is a common put-down. Often feeling completely isolated, these youth must make a perilous journey to adulthood through a society which provides them with only negative feedback. As one seventeen-year-old lesbian explained in her testimony before the Commission:

There is one difference that sets sexual minorities apart from other minorities—we can be invisible, and are assumed to be a part of the heterosexual majority until we declare otherwise. I tried that for a while, going so far as to use a guy to prove to myself that I could be straight if I tried hard enough. But instead of being accepted into the mainstream, I lost my self-respect.

I felt completely isolated from my friends and family. It appeared that I was the only one who ever had these ''queer'' feelings. I couldn't come out to anyone, because surely they wouldn't want to be friends with anyone as sick and deranged as I.

This initiated a downward spiral of self-hatred and anger motivated by homophobia. I hated myself for seeming to be everyone's worst nightmare—a homosexual. I was angry because no matter what I did I couldn't change that. I was angry because it seemed that I could never be happy. I was angry because I felt I had no right to be angry. I created impassable walls, shutting out love as well as hate. I grew increasingly cynical, trying to stave off hurt, because I felt no one would try to see the person behind the sexual label. I virtually branded myself with the message, ''Stay Back!''

The isolation this student so eloquently portrays puts gay and lesbian youth at high risk for a variety of problems, including:

1. *Violence.* According to the U.S. Department of Justice, ''Homosexuals are probably the most frequent victims'' of hate crimes. Gay/lesbian youth are hardly immune to this society-wide phenomenon: a survey by the National Gay and Lesbian Task Force found that 45% of gay men and 25% of lesbians reported being harassed or attacked in high school because they were perceived to be lesbian or gay. This was illustrated by the testimony of a twenty-year-old college student who testified about the experience he and his best friend shared in high school:

We were shunned by many of our classmates for being, as many saw us, just plain weird. . . . We were also picked on. We were called queer and faggot and a host of other homophobic slurs. We were also used as punching bags by our classmates just for being different, something that sent us into further isolation.

2. *Verbal Abuse.* It comes as no surprise to any teenager or high school teacher that gay/lesbian students are often subjected to verbal abuse. Comments like ''fag'', ''dyke'', and ''that's so gay'' are used so regularly in high schools (often even by teachers) that few even notice such

hateful language as being anything out of the ordinary. According to a survey conducted by the Commission, 97% of students at one suburban high school had heard homophobic language used in school. Another Commission survey found that 43% of students said they heard such language "often," 51% "sometimes," and only 6% say "never." Finally 53% of the students surveyed said they had heard teachers use such language. As one student put it, "I was called *faggot* so much that there were times that I thought this was my given name."

Few teachers sympathetic to gay youth feel able to intervene to stop such harassment for, as Kathy Henderson, a teacher at Phillips Academy (Andover) put it, "Most teachers, gay or straight, are afraid to speak up when they hear homophobic remarks. They're afraid people might say, 'What are you—gay?' which remains a frightening question in today's climate."

3. *Homelessness.* Many families react badly when they find out one of their children is lesbian or gay. A University of Minnesota study found that 26% of young gay men reported being forced to leave home because of conflict over their being gay. An eighteen-year-old gay male testified:

> I remember back in high school, before I dropped out, feeling really out of place and alone. I never quite understood why I felt so different. I didn't withdraw from anything—in fact, I was kind of popular, playing on the soccer team and all . . . (but I felt my feelings were) so wrong, like there was something wrong with me, and I just couldn't handle it anymore. I had nowhere to go no one to talk to.
>
> When I did confide in a school counselor, she screwed my life up. She went back to my parents and told them all these things I had been saying. I never told her I was gay because to me being gay meant you put on lipstick and wore dresses because that's all you ever see on T.V, and I never thought that was me.
>
> I got kicked out of my house in July. There was violence involved. My mother came at me with an iron, and I called the police. The police came, and my mother told them I was always in Boston with fags and that I'm doing this and doing that. The policeman started to crack all these fag jokes and told me what he would do if his kids were gay and told me that I should just leave. I said, "Where am I supposed to go?

4. *Substance Abuse.* Under such stress, many gay/lesbian youth turn to alcohol or other drugs to escape from their problems. The above-cited Minnesota study also found that 58% of the young gay men surveyed

could be classified as having a substance abuse disorder. As a seventeen-year-old gay male put it, "I've spent more than one lonely night sobbing while downing shot after shot."

5. *High Drop-out Rates.* The U.S. Department of Health & Human Services found that 28% of gay youth drop out of high school altogether, usually to escape the harassment, violence, and alienation they face at school. In her testimony, a sixteen-year-old lesbian explained the discomfort that caused her to contemplate dropping out:

> I think what has changed for me the most because of coming out has been school. It is not a place where I can feel comfortable being gay, so therefore I cannot feel comfortable being myself. In the past year my life has become extremely unstable. My attendance at school has fallen steadily, and school has become a place I no longer want to be. I'm scared of the confrontations I may run into because I'm about to start basketball season. Basketball has been the love of my life since I was a small child, and I could never imagine not playing. But recently thoughts of not going out for the team have been very strong. I have spent the last two seasons ignoring homophobic comments made on the team, and I have even laughed along with them at times. Things are different now, because they know I'm gay. Will the comments and jokes end? Will I have to endure the pain of walking into a room that's noisy and having it suddenly fall silent upon my entrance.

This student dropped out of her high school three months after giving this testimony.

6. *Suicide.* Often, gay/lesbian youth feel so hopeless that ending their lives feels like the only solution to their problems. According to the U.S. Department of Health and Human Services, gay and lesbian youth are two-to-three times more likely to *attempt* suicide than heterosexual youth (with 500,000 attempts in the U.S. annually). Up to 30% of *successful* teen suicides each year are by lesbian or gay teens (1,500 out of a total of 5,000 deaths). Using the Departments statistics, this means that a gay/lesbian youth tries to kill him or herself every thirty-five minutes in the United States, and that a gay/lesbian youth succeeds in killing him or herself every six hours. The twenty-year-old college student quoted on violence above testified about the tragic denouement to the story of his best friend:

> Just when it seemed he was beginning to accept himself as a gay man, he hit rock bottom. . . . Richard would frequently come to

U-Mass for concerts and to visit. But when he arrived that night in November, 1989, there was something different about him. He wasn't glad or joking to be in Amherst like he usually was when he came to visit me. He was quiet, and there was no spark in his eyes. When I asked him what was wrong, he simply shook his head. Eventually, with tears in his eyes, he told me he'd been badly beaten up. When I looked closely, I could see that he'd tried to cover a black eye with make-up.

He said as he was leaving the Athol (a small town in rural western Massachusetts) Public Library earlier that week, two people were waiting for him in the back seat of his car. He didn't see them as he got in ready to make the five-minute drive back to his parents' house. An arm came out of the dark, pulling Richard's neck tightly against his seat. Another arm came out of nowhere and began punching his ribs. Defenseless and scared, he could do nothing as he was beaten in his own car. When it was over, he was too ashamed to go home because his parents would see his black eye and his bloody nose, so he drove around in pain. He said he had no idea who beat him. The only word his attackers had said was *faggot.* . . .

My sister called me three days after Christmas this year . . . She told me Richard had driven his maroon Ford Escort to a deserted Athol street and left the engine running, killing himself. I didn't understand why. There seemed to be no reason for his death and for weeks after it, I, like much of his family, was inconsolable.

It has been five months since his death and I just hope that Richard has found a place where he can be himself without being picked on and beaten up. Most of all I hope he's happy.

The picture that emerged after these hearings called for immediate action, and in February, 1993, the Education Committee released its report, *Making Schools Safe for Gay & Lesbian Youth*, which outlined the problems of gay youth and offered a plan of action for schools to follow. Although over seventy pages long, the report's key recommendations can be summarized in six concise points:

1. School policies protecting gay and lesbian students from harassment, violence, and discrimination.
2. Training teachers/counselors/educators in issues relevant to the needs and problems of gay and lesbian youth, including protecting them from harassment and violence as well as drop-out and suicide prevention.

3. Establishment of school-based support groups on the "Gay-Straigh. Alliance" model pioneered by independent schools.
4. Provision of gay-positive, school-based counseling for gay youth and their families.
5. The development of library collections which provide accurate information on gay and lesbian people.
6. The development of curriculum which incorporates gay and lesbian themes and subject matter into all disciplines in an age-appropriate fashion.

The Commission saw these recommendations as the bedrock for building inclusive school communities that allow gay/lesbian students to receive the education they deserve. Fortunately, the Massachusetts State Board of Education agreed, and voted unanimously to adopt the first four points recommended as state policy for all schools in May, 1993. (Recommendation #5 and #6 were not brought before the Board of Education at that time, pending the development of appropriate bibliographies and discipline-specific guidelines on which the Commission is at work.)

Fortunately, the Commission's Recommendations are not abstract concepts but based on programs which have been modeled successfully in both independent and public schools. A case in point has been the "Gay-Straight Alliance" program.

Begun first in the late 1980s at Phillips Academy (Andover) and Concord Academy, Gay-Straight Alliances are student-run clubs, with faculty advisors, where issues of sexual orientation and homophobia are discussed. A cardinal rule is that no one must declare his or her sexual orientation to join, in order that it be a "safe place" where no students will feel put on the spot. These groups have sponsored educational programs, social events, and policy changes which have dramatically bettered the climate for gay students in their schools. This model has spread beyond the first schools to include such prestigious schools as Newton South, Brookline High School, Cambridge Rindge & Latin, and Chapel Hill (N.C.) High School.

Some schools have replied to these initiatives with responses like, "There are no gay students at my school" or "We don't have these kinds of problems here." The first reply is simply factually inaccurate: relying on everything from conservative estimates to the Kinsey Report, gay/lesbian people represent anywhere from 5–10% of every population, which means that every school is dealing with a sizable number of students facing these issues. Not to serve these students reveals professional and ethical irresponsibility. Imagine if suddenly each of our schools had a population of non-English-speaking Chinese language students, who were experiencing significant difficulty with academic success, social adjustment, and retention. We would move swiftly to try to meet their needs. There is no excuse not to do the same for gay/lesbian students. It is our professional responsibility to help each student to achieve to the best of his or her ability, regardless of the student's sexual orientation or our personal feelings about that orientation. That's our job, and doing our job is not optional.

The second reply—"We don't have these kinds of problems here"— only reveals the depth of the problem the school has. The silence in many schools around gay/lesbian issues (which is usually only interrupted by the use of homophobic epithets) is a sign in itself of tremendous anxiety and even terror among the school's gay/lesbian population. Given the fact that each school has gay/lesbian students and staff, we *should* be hearing about gay/lesbian concerns. If we aren't, in all likelihood, it is because the climate of fear is so intense that these individuals are too terrified to speak out. Often in diversity work we mistake silence for contentment, and absence of visible conflict for harmony. In the case of gay/lesbian issues, nothing could be further from the truth. As the button reads, "Silence-Death."

The word *revolution* is not hyperbole when it is used to describe recent developments with regard to our understanding of gay/lesbian youth and their needs. Fortunately, the work of New England-area schools (many of them independent schools) has given us a start toward meeting the needs of this long neglected population. The Massachusetts Governor's Commission on Gay & Lesbian Youth has built on this work to give us a blueprint for how to bring about the changes we must institute if we are to claim that we truly serve *all* of our students. No school can claim to be a "good school" if it ignores the needs of its students. The sooner we address the needs of gay youth, the sooner these students will feel free to become full members of our school communities. Only then will they receive the equal educational opportunity they deserve.

Conclusion

The Culture of the School

by *John Ratte, Head of School*
The Loomis Chaffee School

The reader of these essays has been presented with reflections on nearly every dimension of the life and work of the independent day school. Skilled and experienced practitioners have put down a wealth of knowledge about how to do it, for every significant "it": from effective marketing, recruiting, and enrolling the new student to the care and feeding of the graduate; from the training and evaluating of teachers to the emergence of the vast horizon of computer-assisted learning; from parent relations to race relations to sexual relations; from the internal matters of student life and discipline to the expanding external dimensions of community service and apprentice learning.

Every essay rings with the specifics of personal experience, knowledge and, above all, reflection. These are not simple recipes abstracted from reports or spun out of theory: they offer both the substance of actuality and the insights which come only from analysis of what has been tried, criticized, revised, and tried again. They are addressed by professionals to professionals, and yet for that very reason they offer the friend of independent schools, as well as the person unfamiliar with them, a chance to see the work from the inside. Every essay is a mine of "how to" practicality. Yet all are nourished from within by commitment to the deep moral and pedagogical perspectives which good school-keeping both demands and fosters in those who serve youth.

Many of the issues raised in this collection are not easy issues. They could be presented as such. Fortunately for the reader, they are not. Michael Gary of Pomfret speaks the truth plainly: "Real dialogue between the races rarely ever takes place. It is for this reason we as educators must not ignore, however draining it may be, the historic opportunity we have to change by encouraging dialogue in the classroom, discussing 'differentness' whether it be race, gender, religion, or class." Similarly, Clint Wilkins is wonderfully plainspoken in matching justice for the teacher and the school in his approach to the painful matter of dismissal: "Always give the teacher the opportunity to respond and improve. Don't do anything irrational, precipitous or capricious. Make sure you have lived up to your word. Bring in legal counsel. And again, leave a paper trail."

These are but two examples of plainspoken thoughtfulness; the same virtues inform the linked essays on the initiation and continuing development of teachers, whose authors face the inescapable root fact of the demands of the calling at the same time that they sketch ways of inspiring and facilitating self-directed renewal. The presence together in one collection of Richard Hawley's blend of research reporting and prescription, Carol Hotchkiss's survey of the social realities which surround the school, Pat Bassett's argument for virginity, and Kevin Jenning's research into and reflections on the experiences of gay and lesbian students, dramatize the range and depth of the intensely conflicted issues of social formation and moral development which simultaneously give greater meaning to, and threaten to overcome, the traditional academic mission of the school.

Taken together, these essays point the reader towards reflection and action on the totality of the culture of the school he or she serves. Perhaps the greatest privilege the independent school can claim is the power to shape its own culture. Selective in admissions; reasonable in its ratios of students to teachers; self-confidently academic, with a definition of intellectual work which embraces the arts as well as the humanities, mathematics and the sciences; proud of its commitment to counseling and to community service and to providing physical education and athletics for all; happily dependent for support on parents and graduates; self-governing under boards of trustees who are true volunteers—these are the things independent schools claim to be, to have. Such schools have the opportunity for coherence, for integrity, in the overall experience of students and teachers and staff members, trustees and parents and graduates. They can aspire to be, each one, a whole greater than the sum of its parts.

We cannot easily decide where to begin, or where to leave off, identifying elements of the life of the school that have the potential both to shape and to express its culture. Words themselves, the ideas and values expressed in words, arrangements of time and space, rules and customs, the basic grouping of human beings into classes and other categories, the assigning of honor and the giving of gifts, the telling of stories—all of these have the potential to express the identity of a community, which is to say the identity that certain persons in the community will it to have, or to appear to have.

Self-study groups preparing for visiting accreditation committees rightly place great emphasis on the school's statement of mission, and do well to root about in the archives or the attic to find Latin mottoes, founding charters, *obiter dicta* of the founders and donors, heads and teachers. Faculties and school administrators haggle over the calendar and the daily schedule at cyclical intervals because everyone dimly recognizes that we express the value we give to something by the amount of time we give to it. "Let's get rid of these tiresome assemblies and give 'prime time' to classrooms because teaching is really what we're all about." ". . . Martin Luther King Day is nothing but a token symbol of our commitment to racial equality if it means nothing more than an assembly squeezed into an ordinary day. Let's make the day extraordinary, and here's how we propose to do it. . . ." "I simply cannot see why I should be expected to cover the same amount of material in a nine-week winter term when I have eleven weeks for that material in the fall and spring terms." ". . . If we want to show the faculty that we really care about them and can really be trusted with the mission of the school, let's at least spend two full days for the Board meeting and make certain that we have that dinner with the whole faculty every fall. . . ." "I know you can't really have a decent conversation with a parent when the conferences are scheduled for only five minutes, but it's only meant to be a symbol of our commitment to respond to their ideas about what we're doing in the classroom; it's really just an invitation to stay in touch with us throughout the year."

And how to overestimate the impact of the organization of space on human thought, action, and feeling as well! Where do people sit and stand and walk? Where do they play and rest? What spaces confine them? What space opens up vistas? How is human movement throughout the day and the week and the term and the school year shaped by corridors and doors and windows and walls and quadrangles and alleys and slopes and fields and the line of the hills or the towers of the city in the distance? What are the ordinary spaces and what are the special spaces? Why can't the seniors have a senior room all to themselves? Why is the upper school on that campus and the lower school on this campus, and what would it mean if we swapped them? Does neo-Gothic architecture mean discipline, meditation and a singular devotion to learning? Does the architecture of the 18th century and of the colonial revival of the early 20th century sym-

214   LOOKING AHEAD

bolize enlightenment, as Jefferson intended in his design for the University of Virginia? Does the steel and glass, pseudo-Bauhaus, semi-industrial architecture of American public and private high schools in the 1950s and 1960s mean that children are production units in the creation of a national work force?

Nothing can create a tradition more quickly than architecture. Consider the New England school built to look instantly as if it were a Cotswold village comfortably hunched down in the valley since the 13th century, with sandblasted thresholds and beams soaked and dried to give roof lines the sag of centuries. Consider the campus of the school that has added to its colonial revival architecture of the 1920s the steel and brick and glass, flat-roofed science center of the 1950s, the new brutalism of reinforced concrete in the 1970s, and now builds a post-modernist neo-colonial dormitory or dining hall or arts facility with limestone columns, slate roofs, and a plethora of Palladian windows. Consider the school that looks at its row of colonial and federal houses and realizes that the best expression of its tradition is to build more school buildings that look like private houses.

The architectural history of independent schools in America is a history of stating and shaping a tradition through the physical organization of space, and then expressing within those spaces the permanence of the identities of those boys and girls and men and women who have associated themselves with the institution. That is why we have the portraits of the chairs of the board of trustees and of the heads; the lists of prize winners and teams and prefects and cum laude members; and, in some schools, a wood carving made by every boy since the beginning. The school asserts itself as a community transcending time and created by people who are presented to us as having no history other than their history at school.

Andy Warhol offers each of us 15 minutes of fame; the school offers us membership in a kind of immortality, through its organized space, meanings expressed in architectural modes, paintings, plaques and lists—all summed up in the (quaint, remote, antique) motto and often in Latin and often in an image. In translation, these phrases seem strangely alike in their concern for character and service. "Do not give way to evil things," "truth," "light and truth," "not for one's self," "not for one's self, but for others," "to minister, not to be ministered unto." Pity the principal or head possessed of any one of these condensed codes of virtue, who does no use it over and over again in order to focus a community's attention on the endless dialectic between the individual seeking his or her own interests and the person accepting and building identity through society and in service to it. Like medieval stained glass, the image has power as great as the words. We read, "They give light to the earth," and we see on the shield the shining sun; we read, "not for one's self," and we see the image of the hive and its busy bees.

Fortunate indeed is the school whose founders, or refounders—for there's no end to the making of traditions, and no time that cannot become the new *ab initio*—themselves possessed, or possess, or can purchase, a deep iconographical sensitivity. Our records do not show who decided to place the bust of the founding headmaster seven and one-half feet above floor level in Memorial Hall (where the marble panel bearing tribute to the founders has flowers before it on every important occasion), but it is perfectly clear that no subsequent head of the school can, literally, "come up to" that man and his now legendary achievements. And this is as it should be; there need be only one George Washington.

And then there is the endless procession of real and imaginary beasts whose symbolism is more subtle and complex. Take, for example, the industrious and humble badger, or the pelican, ready to wound itself to feed its young, who peers down at us from the pediments above doorways mutely saying, "How far will you go in giving of yourself?"

Since we are playful creatures, we want to be delighted by the richest possible vocabulary in what we speak and hear and see; families and prospective students visiting the gothic, neo-classical, colonial, colonial revival, Spanish missionary, and neo-Spanish missionary campuses—public and private, collegiate and secondary—do not really think that they are entering into the historical period expressed in volume and mass and surface; but neither do they think that they are in mad King Ludwig's castle when they go to Disney Land or Disney World. What they do want is order and intentionality.

Here's the question: Can poverty and makeshift have as much empowering order and intentionality as the complex iconographies of wealth and privilege? The small, new independent school, renting quarters in the Parish House, its modest possessions carefully stored every night in bookcases and rolling boxes built for the purpose by fathers and mothers eager to donate their time and the materials; the storefront school, with its scrubbed floors and faded blackboards and walls covered with student work and teachers' projects; the expanding middle school, with classrooms in rented Butler buildings and a carefully developed long-range plan for material and physical growth as an expression of community and participation, and not a penny to realize it?

I think the answer must be *yes*. Every institution has the possibility and the obligation to create its tradition and embody its symbols, its two- and three-dimensional icons, but principally its icons of word and deed, in order to make more fully possible that modeling of interdependence and of self-discovery and self-making in society that is the school's principal moral responsibility.

Listen to the kids; they know all about this. They watch carefully to see what the favorite teacher eats and wears and how he drives, and how he comforts himself when the team loses the decisive game. They deride the chapel requirement and mock the assembly talks and later reminisce with awkward eloquence about the old tree seen changing with the seasons through the chapel window. They argue over the assembly that linked some crisis of the school with some issue in the larger world.

But more importantly, watch how they make their own traditions and symbols, now in a friendly, now in a contentious dialectic with the symbols and traditions given to them by the grown-ups. Their special ways of doing things are comparatively evanescent; some last a term, some a year, some a whole student generation. They are the expressions of the same space-organizing, turf-claiming, time-grasping, myth-making drives that shape the little world of their school at its retrospectively magic moment of founding five, 50, or 150 years ago.

Much of this symbolic culture and its instant traditions is of necessity hidden from us, though we see expressions in changing styles of dress, and always in music—especially those of us who are young enough to have a kindred taste and know something about how a generational worldview is expressed and then changes through popular music. The closer students are wanting for themselves the traditions and symbols of the middle class, and the more likely it is that their inherited economic advantages will guarantee them their share; then, the more readily they join that version of reality; at the opposite extremes, street gangs invent entire worlds of meaning and express them with iconographic originality and force in special speech, rules and codes of behavior, dress and dreaming.

The harsh facts of class and culture dominate the making of tradition, but they do not restrict it, reminding us that traditions and symbols in any society, including the school, are tools of power, leadership, decision. The right attitude on all of this is one of irony, not cynicism. We are all media savvy; we all know that a Ralph Lauren ad campaign offers instant membership in the WASP aristocracy, or a particular perfume could entitle you to all the trappings of imperial rule. In our world there exist "real" castles, Ludwig's imitation and Disney's double ersatz; there are real fragments of the past in Massachusetts and Virginia, as well as Colonial Sturbridge and Colonial Williamsburg; there are real alligators in their natural home, real alligators in their artificial home in the amusement park, and then there are mechanical alligators in Tokyo where real ones cannot survive. The "tradition" of the popular British monarchy is the invention of the 20th century, just as the tradition of Ronald Reagan's America is the invention of media specialists in the 1980s. For the Briton, the Union Jack is something that can be worn on the pants and purchased as a dish towel; for some Americans, Old Glory is an object as sacred as the Grail. What is certain is not the definition of tradition, or how it will be used or abused, but the inescapability of the obligation to invent it, and to be invented by it as well.

As the phenomenon of Communism in the 20th century fades, as the symbols of the USSR become the sought-after decorations on American T-shirts, as fragments of the Berlin Wall gain in value on the collectors' market, we are struck as much by the rich and elaborate tradition that was created by the Bolshevik iconographers and symbolized by those images of Stalin and Lenin, now on their way to the foundry, as we are by their successors' fading power. As Communism as a community fades, nationalism and its symbols resurge; yet there must be some tradition because in every useful human institution there must be some expression of the contract Edmund Burke saw linking the dead, those of us who are alive today, and generations yet unborn.

The healthy school, whether public or private, is no different from any other community of men and women in its need to express its controlling ideas through language, through the organization of time and space, and through the hierarchies it establishes in order to carry out its work. We have talked about mottoes and mascots, rules and regulations, and architectural configurations, and it remains for us only to consider what is perhaps the most dominant and inescapable and creative expression of the myth of a school, and that is the storytelling that the institution generates over time.

It is not the mark of mythic poverty for a school to lack a towering campanile, a Gothic cloister, a neo-colonial colonnade, or a school blazer, but it is poverty and death for a school to lack good stories about its people, their achievements and their failures. At the heart of a school's myth is the cluster of dominant stories that everyone knows and tells over and over again, and then the infinite collection of new tales that attach themselves like so many lesser stones around the central diamond, light reflecting light. Although the building blocks will be the same for every school, the central tale, the core story in the myth, will be unique to that institution. The founders names will be unique, the descriptions of the first generation of teachers, the particular sequence in which buildings were built, the crisis of the bank loan, the challenge of getting the first accreditation certificate, and the like, will all be special, our story, the way we did it, and unlike the way anybody else has ever done it.

Matching, though opposite, is the quality of generality and sameness in all the other stories that nourish the life of the school. Every school will have its legendary coach, its unsurpassed classroom eccentric who caught his students' attention with an unerringly aimed piece of chalk, its fabled registrar who kept all the information in her head and, when she retired, was replaced by four clerks (and when the tale is told today, it will be two computers). What matters is that these tales, and the negative ones as well—the cast party that got out of control, the teacher who could not win the battle with the bottle—what matters is that all these tales constitute a family of legends that school people can recognize and share, at home and away from home.

What intrigues us so much is the simultaneity of uniqueness and sameness in the school, be it public or private. After all, these are places where boys and girls learn and men and women teach, and the practices common to the profession of teaching and to the work of learning must be universal, whatever the variations of language, technique and technology. How we love to hear the stories of our colleagues returned from an exchange year in Australia or India as they show us the very same thing done in an utterly different way. Through the sharing of stories, we come to think of our school as a true universal because the combination of its central and unique tale of founding and continuation, and its multiple human stories so similar to those of other creatures in other institutions, when taken together, constitute the ultimate symbol, the thing that links together mysteriously the past, the present and the future. In order to be truly ourselves in a school—or I should say, in order to discover what we truly are, and make it at the same time—we must be simultaneously special and common, utterly singular and truly plural, inextricably bound up with a certain landscape, a certain language, a certain set of practices, and yet at the same time spaceless, timeless and all-encompassing.

Why do we love to play games with other schools?—because there we see ourselves most uniquely, even as we see our brother and our sister. Why should it matter so much that a pelican triumph over a badger, or a griffin over a gargoyle?—because we know who we are, gathered around by totem, because we are testing ourselves when we wrestle with our near-double in the kingdom of learned animals. Thus do we recognize and make our world through the symbols of our loyalty to each other and of our passion to do the work well.